IT Services Leadership Handbook

A Practical Guide for Project, Program, Service Delivery & Practice Managers

By

Bhaskar Challa

Copyright © 2025 Bhaskar Srinivas Challa

All rights reserved

No part of this book may be reproduced, or stored in a retrieval system, or transmitted in any form or by any means, electronic, mechanical, photocopying, recording, or otherwise, without express written permission of the author.

Disclaimer: The information provided in this book is for general informational purposes only. The author and publisher assume no responsibility for errors or omissions. The reader is encouraged to seek professional advice as needed.

ISBN 9798324787097

Dedicated to all the Leaders who helped shape my professional career. A Big Thank You!

Contents

Foreword

Chapter 1: Introduction to IT Service Leadership

Chapter 2: Self-Assessment

Chapter 3: Challenge as an opportunity

Chapter 4: Leadership Styles

Chapter 5: Leadership Traits

Chapter 6: Project Management Leadership

Chapter 7: Project management Challenges

Chapter 8: Project management Practical Solutions

Chapter 9: Program Management Leadership

Chapter 10: Service Delivery Management Leadership

Chapter 11: Service delivery management challenges and solutions

Chapter 12: Practice Management Leadership

Chapter 13: Practice Management challenges and solutions

Chapter 14: AI Prompt Engineering

Chapter 15: Analytics, Automation & AI Ops

Chapter 16: Conflict resolution

Chapter 17: Communication Skills: Non-Verbal

Chapter 18: Communication Skills: Verbal

Chapter 19: Time Management

Appendix: Noble Virtues

Foreword

"True leadership is forged through experience, not a gift at birth"

Early in my IT services career, I faced a challenge as a database administrator. Our database size surged, surpassing the first alert level of 60% and projected to hit the critical 80% threshold within a month. This was in a pre-cloud era, requiring physical procurement of storage and servers.

Following protocol, I informed my manager. As financial approvals were needed, it escalated to a senior management call. While preparing, I reviewed our inventory and discovered unused storage space.

At the meeting, I presented the situation and mentioned the available storage. Our service delivery director, a highly respected leader, acknowledged it, but explained it was reserved for future growth. He then made a request for additional storage to address the immediate need with the finance team.

Given his seniority, I initially hesitated to disagree. Believing he might have missed my point; I politely restated the existing storage. He smiled and clarified. The existing storage was strategic planning for future growth for the next 2 years – this unexpected spike required separate resources.

Then came the leadership principle that resonated deeply: *"'We cannot steal from our future.'"*

This was a powerful lesson. While I focused on the immediate issue, the senior leader had a broader vision, already planning for future needs. He was not overlooking my point; he was demonstrating long-term thinking.

This experience was a masterclass in practical leadership. Observing his handling of various situations, I became convinced he was a natural leader. When I told him so, he gave a painful laugh and replied, 'I wish that were true.'

Working in leadership roles and observing others taught me that leadership is crafted through experience, both personal and learned. I came to understand that leadership is fundamentally shaped by experience—both our own and that gained from others. This process frequently involves navigating challenging, even painful, situations.

This simple book dispels the myth of the "natural-born leader and through real-world examples you will gain a deep understanding of The Four Major IT Service Delivery Leadership roles and the specific challenges faced by leaders in IT service organizations.

Individuals in, or aspiring to, leadership positions such as project, program, service delivery, and practice managers would find this book advantageous.

Chapter 1: Introduction to IT Service Leadership

The Symphony of IT Service Delivery

Information technology (IT) has become the backbone of modern business success. All modern business organizations either have an internal IT department or outsource to IT service organizations. The pervasive reliance on technology has fuelled the explosive growth of the IT services industry.

To effectively manage their day-to-day operations, businesses are pursuing various IT strategies. These include building strong internal IT departments, establishing Global Capability Centres (GCCs), or outsourcing to managed service providers (MSPs), value-added resellers (VARs), and system integrators (SIs).

While strong technical expertise remains essential, modern IT service organizations require leaders with strategic thinking, business acumen, and exceptional communication skills. They must be adept at building and motivating high-performing teams, navigating change with agility, and forging strong partnerships with both internal and external clients.

IT service delivery leadership is a complex ecosystem requiring a well-coordinated team to deliver successful outcomes. Each role plays a distinct part, contributing to the overall symphony of service excellence.

1. The Conductor: Project Management

Project managers are the meticulous conductors of individual IT projects. They orchestrate the delivery of each project within predefined parameters of schedule, budget, and scope. They act as the central point of contact, leading a team of specialists and ensuring efficient resource allocation. Project managers constantly monitor progress, proactively identify, and mitigate risks, and ensure all project activities contribute to the final deliverable. Their success hinges on their ability to maintain clear communication with stakeholders, adapt to changing circumstances, and deliver projects that meet agreed-upon expectations.

2. The Maestro: Program Management

Taking a broader perspective, program managers act as the maestro, overseeing a coordinated group of interconnected IT projects. Their focus is on ensuring these projects align with the organization's larger strategic objectives. Program managers prioritize projects based on their importance to the overall program goals. They allocate resources efficiently across the entire program, ensuring alignment and minimizing conflicts. They also monitor program-level risks and dependencies, proactively identifying potential roadblocks and implementing measures to keep the program on track. Program managers provide high-level direction and guidance to individual project managers, fostering collaboration and ensuring each project contributes to the overall program's success.

3. The Engine Room Crew: Service Delivery Management

Service delivery managers are the engine room crew, the unsung heroes who keep the IT infrastructure running smoothly. They are responsible for the day-to-day operations of delivering IT services to end-users. They meticulously implement and maintain service delivery processes, ensuring a consistent and high-quality service experience. This includes adherence to service level agreements (SLAs) that define the expected level of service for various IT offerings. Service delivery managers oversee the service desk, the first line of contact for user inquiries and issues. They manage incident resolution, ensuring prompt and efficient troubleshooting of any problems that arise. Additionally, they handle problem management, proactively identifying recurring issues and implementing preventative measures to minimize downtime and ensure service continuity.

4. The Coaches: Practice Management

While the other roles focus on project execution and service delivery, practice managers act as the orchestra's coaches, constantly striving to refine and improve the organization's IT service delivery practices. They champion continuous improvement, analyzing and identifying best practices in areas like ITIL frameworks, automation tools, and service management methodologies. Their role involves implementing these practices to optimize service delivery processes and enhance efficiency. Practice managers ensure the service delivery team has the necessary skills and knowledge to deliver high-quality services. They organize training programs, encourage knowledge sharing within the team, and stay abreast of industry trends to ensure the team embraces the latest advancements in IT service delivery. Practice managers work with the sales, presales & delivery teams in putting together proposals to acquire additional business.

What to expect

My transformation from an employee with technical experience to management roles has been a tough one. I was lucky to have excellent leaders who guided me from time to time, but most of the learning has been through day-to-day experiences. I have been fortunate to work in each of the four roles that are discussed in this book.

The transfer of knowledge across generations is something unique to human species. We can learn from our forefathers, and contemporaries.

You do not need to acquire the knowledge only through the actual experience. But also, through the experiences of others.

This book also helps with personal leadership development. Leadership styles, Leadership traits & virtues, Verbal & Non-Verbal communication skills, and Time management are all covered.

I hope the experiences shared along with the information works as a comprehensive leadership handbook for IT service leaders.

Chapter 2: Self-Assessment

No one knows us better than ourselves. Self-assessment is a crucial step in understanding career goals. By gaining insights into yourself, you can make informed decisions in your leadership journey.

We will use SWOT Analysis, a self-assessment tool that focuses on strengths, weaknesses, opportunities & threats for personal development, career planning, and business strategy.

The SWOT Analysis

Strengths are the things that you do well. They are the things that make you unique and valuable.

Weaknesses are the areas where you need to improve. They are the things that hold you back from achieving your goals.

Opportunities are the external factors that could help you to achieve your goals. They are the trends and changes in the world that you can take advantage of.

Threats are the external factors that could hinder your ability to achieve your goals. They are the challenges and obstacles that you need to overcome.

Instructions to fill out questionnaire

If you are using the paperback book, you can directly fill in the data into the space provided. If it is an online version ebook that you are reading, make note in a separate book. Do not keep the responses just in your mind. Be honest, Be specific. Be realistic. Be comprehensive.

- Find a quiet corner at home before starting.
- Fill in this sheet with a pencil so that you can make any changes later.

Questionnaire1: Personal SWOT Analysis

Task	Response
What are my top 3 strengths?	
What are my top 3 Weaknesses?	
What are my top 3 Opportunities?	
What are my top 3 Threats?	

Chapter 3: Challenge as an opportunity

Who will run faster?

- A-Someone jogging in the morning
- B-Someone being chased by a dog

Who will choose healthier food filled with nutrition?

- A-Someone not in shape, but young
- B-Someone warned by a doctor, that their life depends on a healthier diet

I happened to meet a friend of mine after 2 years. He lost 40kg (90 lbs). It was remarkable seeing him so fit. I asked him to share the secret, felt like he had cracked the code.

He lost his dad who was obese due to COVID-19, whom he loved very much, and the personal trauma of the incident transformed him. He decided on that day, not to have his immediate family suffer a similar fate ever again. He decided to lead a healthy lifestyle.

A Professional story

A few years ago, I was hired to work on a mission critical project at a top Organization.

Joining the company was a whirlwind. After a quick orientation, I was thrown into a high-pressure situation. On my second day, a critical system outage, caused by human error, had the team reeling. The project's fate hung in the balance. I had not even received my laptop, let alone had time to understand the team or project.

My initial customer introduction, meant for pleasantries, became a crisis management meeting. I said, 'I wish we were meeting under better circumstances. Let me present the analysis and our corrective action plan. We propose a 90-day recovery, with a comprehensive report in three days.' The customer's response was positive.

The following three days were intense, developing the plan, followed by a challenging 90-day execution period. Despite the stress, we succeeded, later leading to a two-year project renewal. This event also helped the customer to trust us better and we received additional business.

Had the crisis not arisen, I am pretty sure we may not have had the additional business and the boost to my own career.

Examples of great personalities & their challenges

These examples are outside the IT world, but I am sure, inspiration can be taken from anywhere.

Professor Stephen Hawking: Diagnosed with ALS at age 21. Though his body started failing, used mental powers to do most of his path-breaking work after the diagnosis of the disease. Hawking himself wrote about finding beauty and meaning in the universe despite his limitations.

Michael Jordan: Cut from his high school varsity basketball team during his sophomore year at Laney High School. This event is often cited as a pivotal moment in his career, fuelling his motivation and dedication to become a basketball legend. He went on to become one of the greatest basketball players of all time after that initial challenge.

Stephen King: A prolific horror writer, King struggled with addiction and rejection early in his career. He persevered and became one of the most successful authors of all time, proving that even dark experiences can fuel creativity.

Dashrath Manjhi: Known as mountain, Manjhi lost his wife to illness at a young age. He felt he could have saved her if not for the mountain standing between his village and the hospital. In her memory, carved a 100-meter path through the mountain working alone for 22 years using just a chisel and hammer which reduced the distance between the Atri and Wazir Ganj in Bihar, India from 55 km to 15 km. The crisis in his life lead to improvement of lives of countless others.

Jadav Molai Payeng: Moved by the plight of dying reptiles with no tree cover, Molai known as the "Forest Man of India" single-handedly planted a 1300-acre forest over 40 years. This forest is now known by his name Molai Forest in Assam, India. It has become home to a variety of wildlife, including elephants, rhinos, tigers and deer.

Covid lockdowns: Students and employees, all had to transition to alternate forms of study & work and succeeded to thrive. They are common people, including you and me. Came out successful after one of the biggest tragedies of our times.

Brief conclusion

While there may be exceptions, it is in our human nature to be motivated to act or transform dramatically only when faced with a challenge or a crisis. Why not use a challenge, be it professional or personal, to make lasting change or transformation and a better and stronger leader?

Chapter 4: Leadership Styles

The success of an Individual, family, organization, or country is dependent on leadership. If I can take it to an extreme, even Survival of these entities depends on leadership.

Ponder over a few of these random names and the impact they had:

Steve Jobs, Abraham Lincoln, Hitler, Alexander, Mahatma Gandhi, Mother Theresa... We can go on, the impact through their leadership for good or bad, is huge.

The simplest definition of leadership: "Guiding people and making them work towards a common Goal"

The biggest question: Can leadership be learned?

Answer: An emphatic Yes! It can be!

However, there is no perfect leadership recipe. The best leadership style will vary depending on the situation, the needs of the followers, and the leader's personality. Effective leaders learn to adapt their leadership style to the situation and get the best out of their followers.

By understanding different leadership styles and developing the key characteristics of effective leaders, you can become a more effective leader yourself. Go through these in detail. Take some time to evaluate yourself. What is your natural style and what are the other styles that you need to learn?

Remember, all below styles are required by a leader. You cannot choose only one and leave the rest. Learn all, and implement a style as per the situation!

Leadership Styles

Authoritarian leadership: Authoritarian leaders make decisions without consulting their followers and expect their followers to obey their instructions. This style of leadership can be effective in situations where quick decisions need to be made, but it can also lead to resentment and low morale among followers.

Democratic leadership: Democratic leaders involve their followers in the decision-making process and seek their input and feedback. This style of leadership can be effective in building trust and morale among followers, but it can also be slow and inefficient in situations where quick decisions need to be made.

Laissez-faire leadership: Laissez-faire or Free-Hand leaders give their followers a great deal of autonomy and freedom. This style of leadership can be effective in situations where followers are highly skilled and motivated, but it can also lead to chaos and confusion if followers are not given enough guidance.

Charismatic leadership: Based on the leader's charm, persuasiveness, and ability to connect with others on an emotional level. Charismatic leaders are often seen as being larger-than-life. They can build a strong following and inspire people to believe in them.

Visionary leadership: Based on articulate a clear and inspiring vision for the future. Visionary leaders can see the big picture and develop strategies to achieve their goals. They are also able to communicate their vision to others in a way that motivates them to action. Visionary leaders make people believe in their vision!

Servant leadership: Servant leaders put the needs of their followers first. They are committed to helping their followers grow and develop. They lead by example and perform a task themselves to show how it is done. Servant leadership can create a positive and supportive work environment where everyone feels valued and respected.

Ethical leadership: Ethical leaders make decisions and act in a way that is consistent with their values and principles.

Effective leaders often use a combination of different leadership styles, depending on the situation. For example, a leader who is typically democratic may need to use a more authoritarian style when making a quick decision in a crisis.

Emphasising for effect again, there is no one perfect style. A leader must adopt a style based on the situation.

Visionary Leadership

Vision is the ability to see the future and articulate a clear and inspiring plan for achieving it. Visionary Leaders have a strong vision for their team or organization. They make people Believe in their vision, and communicate that vision in a way that motivates them to action.

Out of all styles of leadership, visionary leadership is my favourite. While you make sure that all the above various leadership styles are used as per the situation, this style should ideally be the long-term goal for yourself. The greatness of this style is that the followers enjoy doing the work for the leader. This is a win-win situation.

There is an interesting study conducted by the University of California, Berkeley.

The study was conducted in a factory that produced car parts. The researchers randomly assigned car factory workers to either a group that would watch a video of how their products were used in cars or a group that would not watch a video. The workers in the video group were shown a 10-minute video that showed how their products were used in different types of cars and how they made the cars safer and more efficient. The workers in the non-video group were given a 10-minute break.

The workers were then sent back to their work which involved assembling car parts. The result was amazing!

The researchers found that the workers in the video group completed the tasks faster and more accurately than the workers in the non-video group. The researchers also found that the workers in the video group were more satisfied with their jobs and more motivated to work hard.

There are a few other similar experiments which confirm this trend

- A study by the University of Pennsylvania found that sales reps who were given a chance to try out the products they were selling were more successful than sales reps who did not have a chance to try out the products.

- A study by the University of Chicago found that employees who were given a tour of the company's facilities were more satisfied with their jobs and more motivated to perform well than employees who did not receive a tour.

- A study by Gallup found that employees who are engaged in their work are more productive and less likely to quit their jobs.

- A study by Glassdoor found that companies with high employee engagement scores have better financial performance than companies with low employee engagement scores.

The above examples show the potential of visionary leadership. If a leader can show the proper vision to his team on what the outcome of their work is, his or her team tends to perform exceptionally.

Synergy

There is a special point here to take note. The leader must find synergies in his vision with that of his follower's needs. That is right, there is some effort needed!

No one commits themselves 100% unless they see benefits for themselves. There is a good amount of background effort before plunging into this mode of leadership. Either as part of appraisals or other discussions, a leader should identify the personal goals and aspirations of his next-level team members.

Communication

The next important point is communicating how the leader's vision benefits his team. Effective communication of this synergy is an Art!

The leader must find synergies in his vision and that of his followers needs.

Example: Assume you are a manager at an IT Services company. You are to deliver a product code and assign team members who do not have the required skills. The team members are to learn and then accomplish this task. If the leader only sets deadlines, may not get the best outcome.

First, identify the team members who aspire to learn, and find synergies of your goal with that of the team members.

Do research on this skill. How important this skill is in the marketplace, advantages it has if one acquires it, etc. Then communicate this information to the team members about how it can personally benefit them. Offer the training. Give them the deadlines.

Synergize & communicate!

Visionary Leadership summary

- Have a clear view of the organization and the specific task goals
- Communicate this vision clearly to your followers.
- Have a visual presentation either through video, audio or PowerPoint. Your vision should be understood clearly.
- Vision need not be only one larger goal. It can be a lot of smaller tasks.
- Do some research, and find synergies of your vision with that of your followers' personal goals. Explain the benefits to them
- Keep an open mind get feedback on your vision and refine it as needed.
- Further, continue this path
    - Read books and articles about vision and leadership.
    - Talk to other leaders about their vision.
    - Write down your vision and share it with others.

Chapter 5: Leadership Traits

I will touch upon the leadership traits with emphasis on how to develop them. These points are from my personal experience so some of them may not exactly suit the textbook definitions.

Think about an experience where you entered a room full of people. You wanted some information. You are not familiar with anyone in the crowd. You observed the group few minutes, then decided to approach a person and to get the details needed. You got the work done. Whom did you choose?

We are somehow drawn to a leader throughout our lives. A child would know whom to approach to get what is needed. A dog very quickly identifies its master. Its behaviour is different with the master and the rest of the family members.

It would feel like the leaders are born with the charisma. But believe me. This is all acquired. Mostly from experiences and a lot of learning.

Be Approachable

You are going to school for the first day and asking for directions to your class. You do not want to be made fun of once you ask the directions. You would make a quick assessment by looking around who is looking decent, well dressed, smiling demeanour. Walking upright, showing confidence. In simple words approachable.

Think about what you would look for when you want to reach out, and try to be that person yourself. This is the first step if you want to be identified as a leader yourself.

Empathy

The word Empathy is relatively young, just a century since coined. You can google this word a bit more.

Empathy is the ability to understand and be able to share others' feelings.

Going back to the example of the first day at school. It is certainly not easy for anyone new to ask for directions, say for a restroom. You would already be embarrassed and do not want to be made fun of. You would like someone to empathise with your situation.

A leader would identify what the other person is going through.

Effective leaders empathize, which allows them to build trust and rapport. If you see such a person again, you will always be happy to see them and trust them.

Ownership

Ownership is the willingness to take responsibility for one's actions and results. This is an important trait that management of any company likes to see while hiring its leaders.

Effective leaders take ownership of their successes and failures. Any team effort if it is success, give it to your team, if it is failure, own it up. I'm not talking about individual success and failures, you should surely claim credit for success if it is individual effort.

Unfortunately, it happens the other way round. Persons who take credit for success and blame others for failure are just insecure managers, certainly not leaders.

There is a sloka in Bhagwad Gita "Karmanye vadhikaresthe…". Do your best work, but not with the expectation of the fruits of the work. Working in a corporate, make your team look good. Make your manager look good. Make your client look like a hero. Make them all look and feel good. Now you would be wondering.

When will I get my due?

True leadership requires no formal recognition. Authentic leaders, driven by ownership, naturally garner respect. History, like the Nobel Committee's oversight of Mahatma Gandhi, often reveals that the absence of awards speaks more to the institution's shortcomings than the leader's.

Story shared by Dr APJ Abdul Kalam

Former Indian President Dr. APJ Abdul Kalam often shared a compelling story about his mentor, Professor Satish Dhawan, Chairman of ISRO. Dr. Kalam was the Project Director for India's inaugural Satellite Launch Vehicle (SLV) program. After a decade of dedicated work, the team prepared for their first launch on August 10, 1979. The atmosphere was charged with anticipation and anxiety.

Tragically, the launch failed. The rocket crashed into the sea, plunging the team into despair. Dr. Kalam, burdened with the weight of responsibility, felt deeply disappointed. Public criticism was swift and harsh.

However, Professor Dhawan's response was extraordinary. He stepped forward and publicly claimed responsibility for the failure. At a press conference, he declared, 'We failed. But I have complete faith in my team. We will succeed next time.'

His unwavering support proved prescient. The subsequent SLV launch was a resounding success. This time, however, Professor Dhawan instructed Dr. Kalam to lead the press conference and announce the triumph. He wanted the team, and Dr. Kalam specifically, to receive the credit they deserved."

This is an event Dr Kalam shared numerous times and available on YouTube. A shining example of Leadership & Ownership.

Assertiveness

There is this scene from my favourite movie Harry Potter and the Deathly Hallows. Hagrid asks Harry, Hermione & Ron's trio to help his Half-brother in case he is incapacitated or unavailable. The challenge is that this brother is a Giant and not of sound mind.

When the trio reaches the forest, the giant grabs Hermione and lifts her into the air.

Hermione bravely confronts the giant, saying, "Put me down. Now!"

The giant is taken aback by the confidence and command displayed, and lowers Hermione to the ground. This is a simple scene, but a good example of what assertiveness is. Worth a watch!

Assertiveness is the ability to communicate your needs and wants clearly and directly with confidence. Effective leaders can be assertive without being aggressive or passive.

A leader should be able to communicate clearly. You can say a polite but firm yes or no when you need to.

Perseverance

Let me give two of my observations.

Observation 1: During my engineering years I had a couple of friends. One is gifted. He would just glance at a book or hear in the classroom and grasp the entire contents. Would watch movies all night and still excel at exams. Not sure how he could do it, he is a born genius.

The other friend is just a guy with normal intelligence. He would strive day and night. He spent 2 hours extra, more than any of us throughout the 4 years, every single day.

By the final year, we would call both "Genius."

Observation 2: My son showed me the channel of a YouTuber who is just horrible at making videos. The comments were awful. But this person would not stop and make a video every single day for years together. The subscriber count and the views to all these videos are so high that, last observed, this person makes good money and living out of the channel.

I, however, still find the videos difficult to watch!

Both are examples of "Perseverance." It is my observation that those who keep working with discipline in life, eventually win.

Every one of us grew up with the hare and the tortoise story. There is a ringing truth. It can take time, but you can win any task that you have set for yourself.

Persevere and you shall win!

Chapter 6: Project Management Leadership

PMI is a leading organization for project management professionals worldwide. It sets industry standards, conducts research, and offers certifications, most notably the Project Management Professional (PMP) credential.

It has a famous book on project management called PMBOK. For a complete comprehensive understanding and certification, I advise all project management professionals to do the PMP certification and read through PMBOK.

This chapter discusses the actual practical challenges faced by a project manager and their resolutions and approach of a project manager from initiation to completion.

Project management methodologies are the established frameworks that guide project managers in leading their teams to achieve project goals. We will discuss the two major approaches.

The Traditional Approach: Waterfall

Imagine a project unfolding in a linear, step-by-step fashion. This is the essence of the Waterfall methodology, the long-standing approach in project management. Waterfall emphasizes a sequential progression through clearly defined phases:

1. **Requirement Gathering:** This phase involves defining project needs and objectives through in-depth discussions with stakeholders.

2. **System Design:** Based on the gathered requirements, a detailed blueprint outlining the project's functionalities and architecture is created.

3. **Development:** The development team translates the design into a working system, following the specifications laid out in the design phase.

4. **Testing:** Rigorous testing ensures the developed system meets all the functional and non-functional requirements defined earlier.

5. **Deployment:** The final system is rolled out to the end-users, marking the official project completion.

The Agile Approach: Embracing Change

Imagine a project team that can adapt its course on the fly, responding to new information and stakeholder input. This agility is the core principle behind Agile methodologies, a collection of iterative and incremental approaches gaining significant traction. Here are some prominent Agile frameworks:

- **Scrum:** Projects are divided into short sprints (typically 2-4 weeks) where teams deliver working functionalities. Daily meetings, sprint reviews, and retrospectives foster continuous collaboration and adaptation.

- **Kanban:** Work is visualized on a Kanban board, with tasks flowing through stages like "To Do," "In Progress," and "Done." Kanban emphasizes continuous flow and limiting work in progress to optimize efficiency.

Clearly defined projects with minimal uncertainty fare well with Waterfall, while Agile shines in complex environments.

Approach to Project Management in IT Services

There are 5 major phases in project management. These may sound academic, but necessary for the reader to have a good understanding.

1. Project Initiation Phase:

1. **Define Project Scope & Goals:** Clearly outline the project's objectives, deliverables, and what constitutes success. This ensures everyone involved is on the same page.

2. **Develop a High-Level Project Plan:** Create a roadmap outlining the major project milestones, timeline phases, and resource requirements. While a detailed plan with specific tasks comes in the next phase (project planning), this high-level plan provides a general direction for project execution.

3. **Resource Allocation:** Identify the people and tools needed to complete each task. Ensure the team has the necessary skills and experience.

4. **Risk Management:** Identify potential risks that could derail the project (e.g., resource availability, technical challenges). Develop mitigation strategies to address them proactively.

2. Project Planning phase:

1. **Work Breakdown Structure (WBS):** Break down the project into smaller, manageable tasks. This creates a roadmap and clarifies the sequence of activities.

2. **Develop a Schedule:** Utilize project management tools like Gantt charts to create a timeline assigning tasks, durations, and dependencies.

3. **Budget Breakdown:** Allocate budget resources to each task or project phase. Consider potential risks and factor in buffer funds for unforeseen circumstances.

4. **Communication Plan:** Establish clear communication protocols. Define how often team meetings will occur, how information will be disseminated, and who the key points of contact are for stakeholders.

3.Project Execution Phase:

1. **Project Kick-off Meeting:** Host a meeting to introduce team members, review the project plan, and answer any questions.

2. **Task Management:** Assign tasks to team members based on their expertise and workload. Utilize project management software for task tracking and progress monitoring.

3. **Regular Communication:** Maintain open communication channels. Conduct regular team meetings and status updates to identify and address any roadblocks early on.

4. **Change Management:** Be prepared to adapt to changing priorities or requirements. Communicate any necessary adjustments to the project scope or budget with stakeholders.

5. **Quality Control:** Establish quality control measures to ensure deliverables meet the required standards.

4. Project Monitoring and Control:

1. **Track Progress:** Monitor progress against the project plan and budget. Identify and address any deviations promptly.

2. **Risk Management (Ongoing):** Continuously monitor potential risks and implement mitigation strategies as needed.

3. **Lessons Learned:** Document lessons learned throughout the project. This valuable information can be used to improve future project management endeavours.

5. Project Closure:

- **Deliverable Completion and Handover:** Ensure all project deliverables are finalized and handed over to the client or designated party.

- **Project Review and Sign-off:** Confirm project completion with stakeholders and obtain formal approvals.

- **Administrative Tasks:** Finalize project documentation, budgets, and contracts. Release resources like equipment and personnel.

- **Post-Mortem Analysis:** Conduct a meeting to discuss lessons learned, successes, and areas for improvement.

- **Documentation Archiving:** Store project documents securely for future reference.

- **Celebration:** Recognize the team's achievements and celebrate project completion.

Chapter 7: Project management challenges

Project initiation is the toughest phase in a project's life cycle. This is also the so-called honeymoon period where everyone is in good spirits, and tend to ignore or brush the risks or issues under the carpet. The issues get prominent after a certain period resulting in failures. The project manager is most vulnerable in this period.

Scope & Timeline

To win a project, sales teams could have included tasks in the scope that are not feasible as per the agreed timelines. The presales teams may have wrong estimations, contributing to the additional scope in the statement of work (SOW). This project may require more resources than allocated in the SOW.

Recruitment

Resources in the context of the Services industry are mostly people. This is the greatest strength and weakness. Assume a project RFP has been floated and an IT service outsourcing organizations wins it.

Staffing the resources before the project start date is always a problem. Except for a few companies many rely on recruiting skilled resources after the project date is confirmed.

The recruitment team may have forecasted to onboard the resources in a month when initially enquired, but in practice it could be 2-month + notice period.

Project Revenue Margins

The customer success manager who in jest to please the customer and have a good relationship, may agree for the customer to interview each of the candidates selected for a fixed bid project. The customer has not approved to onboard resources with lesser work experience. Senior personnel were not budgeted. This would increase the resource hiring costs. Margins could start taking a hit.

Quality of selected team

The interview panel may not have been rightly apprised on the project roles. Or the hired resources were not up to the mark.

The contract resource hired by the organization is already working at multiple locations and has no time for the project manager. This is a recent trend called Moonlighting! A new problem arising out of work-from-home phenomena.

And then there are *Staff Resignations, Health issues, emergencies & many more!*

All of these come out after the project is officially signed and the project manager has taken over! Let me share some of the experiences and practical solutions.

Chapter 8: Project management solutions

I remember going into an internal management call. This was a week into the new project assignment. The estimations were grossly wrong, which meant the SOW itself was faulty. The project would not make any profit!

I was coming up with all kinds of mitigation plans. Our senior leader asked me to hold on to my thoughts. He then turned his attention to the practice & sales leaders who prepared the SOW and pointed out: "You are setting up the project manager for failure. Get back with a solution in 2 days. Do not involve the project manager to find the solution."

There is a valuable lesson here. Do not try to solve all problems yourself and take all the stress. For any issues that arise, make sure you start reaching out to the senior leadership teams.

Seek Help!

In another instance, the customer wanted to do all the interviews of the team members selected even though the project was a fixed bid. The sales team promised they would allow that. I reached out to the customer success manager who is new and inexperienced. He did not want to offend the customer and has instead put pressure on the team to find resources who are low cost but high in experience. After a month, there was no person onboarded and noticed by both our internal and customer management teams and all ended up in an escalation call.

I explained the issue, and the customer manager, said, you could have escalated this a month ago, I would have sorted it by either giving additional funding or asking the team to not do the additional screening!

That is right, why did I not do it? When we are in the thick of things, we miss the bigger picture. Do not work alone. Ask and you shall be given! If not given, of course must fight for it. But certain seek help.

Lessons Learnt, Risk Register or Issue log

The best way to address issues coming out of project initiation is by maintaining a risk register. The project manager should seek the lessons learnt or risks encountered by similar projects of the organization and should prepare this risk register.

There should be prioritization and owner for of each one of the risks. If it is a sales issue, the owner should be sales, if it is a recruitment issue, the owner should be the HR recruitment manager. Each of the persons should be made accountable and responsible to help you fix the issues.

Escalation calls

There is a need to setup escalation calls internally; to discuss and seek updates (daily, weekly, whichever time frame is based on the urgency) from all the stakeholders. Involve your manager, if there is not sufficient response.

The project manager cannot always be a very nice person. Must be making a lot of noise, the right kind of it.

Communication

Have a Daily and weekly call with the project's internal team members.

Have Weekly, Monthly & Quarterly governance calls including all the internal & customer stakeholders.

After any call, have minutes of the meeting (MOM) sent. Do not consider sending MOM as additional work. You are marking leadership teams in these mails, if there is someone's name against an action item, they will be compelled to act and respond. That is how a project manager gets his work done!

Relationship with manager

Have a weekly connect with your manager, providing with all the accomplishments, issues & updates. Some managers may not have a structured connect, but it is in your interest, to seek it, and provide the updates and help you need. Wherever support is needed, take their help so that they can escalate on your behalf.

Networking with Peers & Support teams

An oft-ignored connect is with peers. You need to know what is going on with all other projects as well. Apart from the structured calls you may have through your manager, do also reach out to them yourself. This need not be a structured meet like weekly calls, it can be more informal. Be in constant touch.

Similarly with all support function heads like sales, Internal IT, recruitment, HR, etc.,

A lot of tasks are accomplished with a personal touch!

Chapter 9: Program Management Leadership

Program management focuses on the coordination and management of a group of interdependent projects towards achieving a common strategic goal. This is distinct from traditional project management, which deals with individual projects.

Program managers navigate the complexities of multiple projects, ensuring alignment, minimizing conflicts, and maximizing the program's overall benefits for the organization. There are 4 major frameworks that are used in program management and you can choose any of them.

Frameworks & Model for Program Management

Project Management Institute (PMI) Program Management Body of Knowledge (PgMBOK) Guide: This comprehensive guide outlines program management best practices, covering program initiation, planning, execution, monitoring, control, and closure.

PRINCE2 (Projects IN Controlled Environments): PRINCE2 provides a structured methodology for program management, emphasizing clear governance, defined roles and responsibilities, and a stage-gate approach for program lifecycle management.

P2M (Portfolio, Program, Project Management): P2M offers a holistic framework that integrates portfolio management with program and project management practices, ensuring strategic alignment across all levels.

Program Evaluation and Review Technique (PERT): **PERT** is a project network analysis technique that helps program managers identify critical paths within the program schedule. By analyzing dependencies between projects, PERT allows program managers to focus on areas with the most significant impact on program delivery timelines.

Approach to Program Management

Program management has all the characteristics of project management. The program life cycle goes through similar phases, from initiation to closure. The standard program management lifecycle is Initiating, Planning, Executing, Monitoring and Controlling, and Closing.

This is the same as project management. Now where does Program management differ?

It is the BIG picture.

The program manager would be able to see the larger picture. A successful program manager should be able to make all the project managers understand the larger context as well.

Internal Program Management

One of the most important calls to be scheduled by a program manager is a weekly call with the project managers. Each of the project managers should present their accomplishments, Challenges, and Ongoing tasks in this meet.

There are several interdependencies in a program. If the individual project managers are aware of the larger picture and empowered sufficiently, the overall workload on program managers goes down significantly.

I have observed that some program managers have a fear of sharing all the information and highly restrict the information sharing. They want the project managers to go through them for every task including communication with their peers. This approach increases the workload of the program manager as they become a bottleneck themselves.

Insist all your reporting managers to copy you in their internal communication so that you are aware of all activities. Never be a bottleneck by insisting on communication going through you.

One of my clients would say "Any amount of over-communication is fine with me. It helps!"

Stakeholder management

Programs often involve a wide range of stakeholders with different interests. Effectively communicating and managing stakeholders throughout the program life cycle is important.

It is better to have an individual connect weekly, either virtual or in person with each of the stakeholders. It is ideal to have a separate communication channel as against the common communication channel for all the stakeholders.

Many tasks get done outside the common governance calls. It is important to forge relationships and socialize one on one.

WBR, MBR & QBR Communication

Weekly Email communication on the overall status of the program and in-person or virtual Monthly & Quarterly business review meets on the status of the program involving all stakeholders is a must.

Before the actual presentation of these business review, make sure you review along with your customer counterpart. You need an ally when you go into the calls and there should not be any disagreements. Any disagreement must be mentioned in the governance call.

Risk Registry

Program managers must maintain a separate risk register for the overall program like the one suggested in the project management chapter.

Program manager should also have a detailed risk management plan for each of the risks. Program managers have larger control and flexibility in preparing and executing the risk management plan as compared to project managers.

RACI (Responsible, Accountable, Consulted, Informed) Matrix

The RACI Matrix defines roles and responsibilities for various program activities. It clarifies who is Responsible for completing a task, who is Accountable for the outcome, who needs to be Consulted during the process, and who should be Kept Informed about progress. A clear RACI Matrix fosters accountability and avoids confusion within the program team.

A program manager must prepare this matrix with defined roles and responsibilities for all stakeholders.

Resource Management-Tough decisions

Projects often compete for limited resources like skilled personnel, budget, and technology. The program manager needs to effectively allocate and manage these resources across all dependent projects.

Programs typically involve multiple dependent projects. Keeping these projects aligned is important. Program managers must make some tough decisions at times to ramp up or down the resources. May also have to scrap a project itself if it impacts the other parts of the program.

Benefits Management

A core principle of program management is focusing on the benefits that the program will deliver to the organization.

A program manager should devise a process for identifying, and measuring the benefits and should be constantly communicating with both internal and external stakeholders.

Some managers are modest. They feel that their actions should speak louder and do not like to highlight achievements, let me tell you, a program manager is a showman or woman. They need to be constantly playing up the achievements and benefits.

Why? You are the motivator in chief for your teams. The slightest of benefits or achievements, play it up. It helps propel further success.

Chapter 10: Service Delivery Management Leadership

Once a project or a program is completed and goes live, a new phase starts where it requires day-to-day support and maintenance of the operations. This is also called IT service management (ITSM).

Service delivery managers strive to maintain service quality while optimizing resource allocation, minimizing costs, and ensuring the business-as-usual activities (BAU).

ITSM & Managed services

ITSM is the **framework or blueprint**. It provides a set of best practices and methodologies for the entire lifecycle of IT services. This includes designing, delivering, operating, and continuously improving them. It ensures a structured and standardized approach to IT service delivery.

Managed services are the **execution arm** that puts the blueprint into action. Managed services refer to a business model where a third-party company takes responsibility for managing an organization's IT operations or other ongoing processes. Managed service providers (MSPs) are the companies that handle these tasks for their clients. They can be specialists in IT services, like network management and security, or offer services in other areas like facilities management or human resources. An MSP will typically have a Service Level Agreement (SLA) in place, which outlines the specific services provided and the performance guarantees.

ITSM (IT Service Management) and managed services are like two sides of the same coin, working together to deliver efficient and effective IT support.

The Guiding Light: ITIL Framework

The IT Infrastructure Library (ITIL) is the primary framework for service delivery management. ITIL offers a comprehensive set of best practices that cover the entire service lifecycle, from design and development to operation and continuous improvement.

The focus is on ongoing service monitoring, measurement, and improvement. Metrics like service availability, incident resolution times, and user satisfaction are continuously monitored to identify areas for improvement and implement corrective actions.

Process Improvement Model: Lean Six Sigma

This model provides a structured approach for analysing, optimizing, and streamlining IT service delivery processes. Lean Six Sigma focuses on identifying and eliminating waste within processes to improve efficiency and reduce errors.

Service desk: Central platform for logging and managing user incidents, service requests, and changes.

IT monitoring: Monitoring the health and performance of IT infrastructure and services, enabling proactive issue identification and resolution.

Configuration management: Track and manage IT infrastructure configuration details, ensuring consistency and facilitating troubleshooting.

*Incident and Problem Management***:** Resolving incidents (service outages) and underlying problems to prevent recurrence.

Reporting: Generate reports on service delivery metrics to track performance and identify areas for improvement.

Automation and AI Integration: Proactive maintenance involves tasks like automated patching, self-healing infrastructure, and AI-powered issue prediction.

User Experience (UX): Integration of User Experience (UX) considerations. Proactive monitoring of user experience metrics and potential pain points.

Cloud Computing: Cloud security, multi-cloud management, and integrating on-premises infrastructure with cloud services.

Cybersecurity: Comprehensive security posture, threat intelligence, vulnerability management, and incident response capabilities.

Chapter 11: Service delivery challenges & solutions

Statement of Work (SOW)

Service delivery management is a very broad area. There would be multiple scenarios where the service delivery manager (SDM) must refer to the SOW quite often. Clients may request activities to be taken care of which may not be in the scope.

For example, SDM and their team could be supporting an application and all the operations 24/7. There may be a request to migrate, upgrade the application, development activities, etc., Traditionally these are not part of the scope, but if not explicitly mentioned in the SOW, could create an issue for the delivery manager.

SOW hence becomes a critical component and the SDM should ideally be part of the initial preparation process or should have a good understanding of what is included during the initial transition process from the presale's teams. What is in scope and what is not in scope should also be included in the SOW.

If not, the SDM after taking over should have a thorough review and have a discussion with the customer and bring up the concerns upfront.

24/7 operations

Service operations are mostly 24/7, 365 days a year. There are multiple challenges due to this round-the-clock model.

- SOW should include estimations for the weekends & holidays

- The holidays could be different for each of the different teams. If the support team and customer team are operating in different parts of the world, the holiday list must be exchanged and communicated ahead of time
- Daylight savings (DST) changes must be accommodated and communicated ahead
- Resource scheduling data should be shared with the customer

Escalation procedure

- It is observed that the high priority & severity issues (called P1 incidents) get raised at most unlikely hours like midnight or holidays.
- There could be junior team members in graveyard shifts (after midnight), weekends or holidays
- Escalation procedure must be established and relevant contact details shared with all the team members and reviewed from time to time
- All team members including junior resources should know whom to call
- Some team members are hesitant to call senior folks, need to be educated!

Resource Management

- **Inefficient staffing:** Staffing projects with the right people and skillsets is crucial but can be difficult. This can lead to delays, errors, and unhappy customers.

- SDM should also check the skills and skill gaps and plan with the Learning & development team to arrange for training for the team members
- SDM must take critical calls on non-performing members if up skilling does not work. Any leniency with team members can cause failure. Remember, you are only as strong as your weakest link.
- Allocate non-performing resources back to the practice or initiate PIP (performance improvement plans).

Automation

Any opportunity to automate a task should be taken up by the SDM. Any repetitive tasks like health checks, alerts, etc should all be converted into automation. Some of these tasks maybe outside the preview of an SDM. But an SDM should always try to acquire this knowledge and influence so that in the longer run, the support operations get smoothened out.

- Self-Service Portals should be considered for routine tasks like password resets
- Repetitive tasks like service provisioning, configuration management, and report generation can be automated, saving time and reducing human error. Tools like ServiceNow can be used for this integration as part of incident creation itself.
- DevOps tools can be used for Automatic infrastructure provisioning
- AI-powered solutions can analyze data to predict potential service issues and proactively address them before they impact customers.

- ML algorithms can learn from past interactions and data to improve the accuracy and efficiency of automated processes.
- Automated chatbots can answer basic questions and route complex inquiries to human agents.

Communication and Alignment

Stakeholder Misalignment: Service delivery needs to be aligned with overall business goals. If there is a disconnect between service teams and stakeholders, it can lead to inefficiencies.

Communication breakdowns: Poor communication between service teams, internal departments, and customers can lead to misunderstandings, delays, and frustration.

There should be a daily internal operations call with the team members in an agile format. Where the day-to-day tasks are discussed and work assigned.

There should also be a weekly internal call to recap the week's events and update the team members with feedback from customers.

Externally there should be 3 review meetings WBR/MBR/QBR. Weekly, Monthly & Quarterly business reviews.

Chapter 12: Practice Management Leadership

Practice management refers to the various tasks and processes that ensure the smooth operation of an IT service business. Depending on the size of the practice, practice managers oversee staff, skill the team and allocate all the resources needed by the team members.

Another important function is growing the IT Service business. The practice manager works with the Presales & sales teams in putting together various Requests for proposals to customers and winning over new business.

The Capability Maturity Model Integration (CMMI) Framework

CMMI is a framework that helps organizations improve their capabilities for delivering quality services. It assesses the maturity of an organization's processes across five key areas: process selection, performance management, process improvement, integrated process management, and supplier integration. By utilizing CMMI, practice managers can identify areas where the organization's service delivery processes can be strengthened.

Practice Management: Tools

Process mapping tools: These tools help visualize and analyze IT service delivery processes, facilitating the identification of bottlenecks and opportunities for improvement.

Data analytics tools: By leveraging data analytics, practice managers can gain valuable insights into service delivery performance, user behaviour, and trends. These insights can inform decisions regarding process improvement initiatives.

Customer Satisfaction (CSAT) Scores: CSAT scores measure customer satisfaction with specific interactions or aspects of the IT service delivery experience. Practice managers utilize CSAT scores to identify areas where they can improve customer concerns and address any pain points.

Net Promoter Score (NPS): NPS measures customer loyalty and willingness to recommend IT services to others. Practice managers use NPS to gauge overall customer sentiment and identify opportunities in conjunction with sales teams

Matrix Structures in an IT Services

A matrix structure is a common way for IT service organizations to organize themselves. It combines elements of two (or sometimes more) traditional structures, typically a functional structure (Practice manager) and a project-based structure (Project, program, or service delivery manager)

The reporting of employees in an organization depends on this matrix structure and it is relevant to a practice manager.

Core Concept

Employees report to two managers simultaneously.

- One manager represents their functional department i.e. Practice Manager (Database, network, cloud, applications, etc.,). This

manager focuses on their skills and expertise within that domain.
- The other manager is typically a project manager who oversees a specific client engagement or project. This manager focuses on delivering that project successfully.

A matrix organization helps with Efficient Resource Utilization, enhanced innovation & improved client focus. The biggest challenge is the potential for conflict. Dual reporting creates friction between project and practice managers!

Variations of Matrix Structures

Weak Matrix: Leans more heavily on the Practice side. Practice managers hold the most power, with project managers having a more limited role in decision-making. Project teams are typically temporary.

Balanced Matrix: Aims for a more equal balance between Practice and project management. Both managers share decision-making authority, and project teams can be temporary or ongoing.

Strong Matrix: Prioritizes project-based management. Project managers have significant authority over resources, budgets, and timelines. Practice managers primarily focus on providing technical expertise and support to project teams. Project teams tend to be more permanent.

A matrix structure can be a powerful tool for IT service organizations when implemented effectively. Each of the organizations uses different matrix structures. For the benefit of understanding the Practice management role better, we will choose the Weak Matrix structure for this chapter, where the Practice manager is all-powerful.

Chapter 13: Practice Management challenges and solutions

Balancing billable hours

In an IT services environment, ensuring staff is utilized efficiently can be a challenge, particularly when projects have variable scope.

Let us take the example of a person who is allocated to a particular project, but the project is not yet signed and the start date is delayed. The sales manager is confident of the SOW being signed and makes a request not to allocate the resource to any other project.

This is a typical problem faced by a practice manager. It is important to track each resource allocation and billing in online or offline mode.

The resource not allocated to any project (referred to as Bench in the IT industry) can be utilized by the practice manager in multiple innovative ways. Have the resource attend training and certifications, have them provide training internal teams, mentoring junior team members, interview panels, automation projects, RFPs, etc.,

The most important point, resources that are not billable are kept idle without any tasks assigned. This is the easiest way to lose a valuable resource. The practice manager has the complete responsibility to keep a resource engaged.

Knowledge Repository

Practice managers are responsible for all the artefacts, tools, and process documents. A good repository with proper access controls must be made available at the individual employee level throughout the practice.

Practice manager with help of the GRC (Governance, Rick & Compliance) teams should keep the repository up to date. All artefacts should be reviewed on a periodic basis to keep them updated and relevant.

Staying current with technology

The IT landscape is constantly evolving. Practice managers need to stay informed about new technologies and ensure staff have the necessary skills to deliver services. Practice managers should work with Learning & development teams in skilling the team members and have them take certifications.

One way to do this is to have compulsory certification as part of the appraisal process.

Apart from the external training, the practice manager should maintain a detailed skill profile of all the employees.

Technology groups

Practice manager can create various technical streams within the practice, arrange by the key skill and nominate skilled persons to lead these groups. These leads do not have any authority, but they use the practice manager's backing to conduct weekly brown bag sessions (knowledge-sharing sessions or training sessions). This will motivate the technically competent resources to give and take internal trainings.

Practice capabilities

Having a good understanding of the services provided and being able to explain to potential customers is an important task for a practice manager. A challenge I have observed is that the services provided by the organization at the practice level are not well defined. If a request for a new proposal arrives, it is important to qualify that proposal by checking the internal capabilities, and skills. No matter what the capabilities are, if every RFP is engaged, it would significantly waste the time and resources of the practice manager.

A solution for this issue is having a well-defined practice presentation (or deck as it is referred to in certain organizations) with the capabilities and services mentioned along with all the major case studies done. For each of the service capabilities, there should be a separate PowerPoint presentation.

The practice manager should arrange each capability area into separate campaigns with help of marketing teams and provide them to the sales teams. If the practice manager is proactive, the RFPs that arrive will be related. If there is no proactive action, sales teams will get proactive and that will hurt the practice with unrelated proposal requests.

Business growth

Scaling the practice to take on new clients and grow the business requires strategic planning and resource allocation. As discussed in an earlier section, this is an important role where the practice manager works with presales, sales, and delivery teams in putting together proposals and presenting to customers to win over new business.

The Sales team may own an RFP, but all the background work is done by the practice manager along with presales teams. Presales team members generally have broad generic skills. A presales person cannot be good at all the capabilities of the organization. The presentation quality suffers and it impacts acquiring the customer.

The solution is for the practice manager to identify strong and competent architect-level resources for each of the service capability areas. There should be a primary and a backup person identified for each of these areas. The practice manager should then allocate this person along with the presales person to work on the RFPs.

CSAT & NPS

Customer satisfaction & Net promoter scores are gathered either quarterly, half-yearly or yearly as per an organizations HR policy. This exercise is generally done during Appraisal cycles. The main purpose is lost as the focus shifts to appraisals and the opportunity to gauge the actual mood of the customer vanishes.

As a solution, the practice manager should have a personal connect with each of their customers after the individual managers have sent the emails requesting this data.

The practice manager should work closely to get the right feedback and coordinate with sales or customer success managers. to get the right data, not the appraisal filling forms. If the right data is available, the growth of the practice can be proactive with right steps.

Remote Resource management

In addition to these challenges, practice managers in IT services may also face issues related to managing remote workforce. There is a bigger problem called moonlighting, where a person remotely working, is involved with more than one organization.

Assuming this is a weak matrix structure, the practice manager will be responsible for the team members working remotely and should have a connect either directly or through a manager. There should be an understanding of the personal situation of all the members in a practice. Whatever privacy advocates say, a practice manager needs to know the personal situations of their employees.

HR teams may have some connect, but day to day connect of an employee is directly with their managers. Their situations influence their work. It is important to maintain healthy relations based on trust so that the employee can share any challenges or issues that could impact their work. This is the only solution for problems like moonlighting, employees not being available during office hours, etc when the teams are working remotely. Have a good personal connect based on trust!

Chapter 14: AI Prompt Engineering

3 shifts and 24/7 operations with a small team of 8 members is a standard format for many service delivery support operations.

I have worked in these operations for many years which impacted my health. From acidity, gastric problems, back pain to carpel tunnel, you name it! Had to put in lot of efforts to get back into the pink of health.

Over the years after my move into management, I was able to improve upon the conditions of some of the teams I managed, largely by leveraging Analytics & automation.

While core principles and frameworks remain essential, leaders need to further leverage the power of AI prompt engineering, AIOps along with Analytics & automation to achieve greater efficiency, proactive problem-solving, and enhanced customer experiences. This will certainly improve the working conditions of the team members.

AI Prompt Engineering

We all know Aladdin's* story: a genie, a magic lamp, and wishes granted. Imagine if that were real—if *everyone* had a genie with such power. It is a thrilling thought, but also a bit unsettling.

In a world where everyone has a genie, who would truly succeed? The answer lies in the ability to articulate clear, effective commands. The person who can best direct their genie will ultimately prevail.

Prompt engineering is a new discipline. It is the art and science of crafting effective prompts or questions.

Recently there was a competition for mobile app development, where the contestants were asked to prepare a application with certain capabilities using AI prompt engineering with least number of commands. The winner created the mobile app within 30 minutes using 6 prompts. Actual development work would have run into weeks.

In this chapter we will explore 9 techniques along with examples. You can use this as an assistant in your management decisions.

1. Zero-Shot Prompting

In this technique, the AI is asked to perform a task without any references. You give only one command to get the work done in this technique and do not reference any other criteria. This is the most common used method currently.

Basic Prompt:

- "Generate a comprehensive outline for a project management plan. "

Adding Specifics:

- "Generate a comprehensive outline for a project management plan. Include sections for Project Overview, Scope, Communication Plan, Risk, Stakeholder, quality and change management"

2. One-Shot Prompting

Here, the AI Model is asked to perform a task by providing a reference.

One-shot prompting for project management plan creation involves providing the AI with a single example of a project management plan or format you prefer. This gives the AI a concrete template to follow, leading to a more tailored output.

"Here is an example of a project plan format I like "<<Copy any draft plan>>".

Now, create a project plan for me using this format, and using following information "<<xx,xx>>."

3. Few-Shot Prompting

In this technique, the AI model is given more than one reference to perform the task. This helps AI to learn from. This allows for a more nuanced understanding of the desired format, style, and content. Here is how it works in the context of resume creation:

"Here are few example resume "<<Resume 1>>, <<Resume2>>, <<Resume3>>".

Now, create a resume for me using the format and style of these resume, using following information "<<my name, email, phone, my experience, my education, my skills>>."

4. Persona prompt

In this technique, we ask the AI to assume a specific personality. AI is asked to believe it is now a specific person. You can assign any personality like a doctor, expert lawyer, software professional, etc.,

This approach is useful for generating contextually appropriate and relevant content.

Example:

"You are a detail-oriented project manager with a strong track record of successful implementations. Please create a project plan for me. My project plan should include managing cross-functional teams and delivering projects on time and within budget. My name is [Your Name] and my contact information is [Your Contact Information]."

5. Perspective prompt

This technique guides the AI to respond from a specific perspective, viewpoint, or angle.

A perspective prompt for project management plan creation involves asking the AI to generate the plan from not yours, but from a customers or employer's perspective.

6. Tablular format prompt.

This prompt generates the data in a table format with rows & columns. AI has this capability and not used much.

Combining a tabular format with a perspective prompt can create a highly structured and targeted resume. This approach is excellent for presenting skills, accomplishments, or project details concisely, while still emphasizing a specific angle.

I am now further combining the perspective prompting and tabular format prompting. This is more complex, but you can surely appreciate the evolution of the thought process.

Example: "You are a recruiter searching for a project manager with proven results. Create a resume for me in a table format. The table should have columns for 'Project Name,' 'Key Accomplishment,' and 'Metrics/Results.' My project experience includes leading cross-functional teams and delivering projects on time and within budget. My education is a Project Management Professional Certification. My name is [Your Name], and my contact information is [Your Contact Information]."

7. Chain of Thought

Now, let us increase the complexity further so that we get better outputs. This is for more advanced users.

In chain of thought prompting, we ask the model to explain its thought process step by step.

Let's say we have a question: "What is 25 multiplied by 5?"

Instead of this question, we pose "solve 25 multiplied by 5 step-by-step. First, breakdown 25 into 20 and 5. Next, multiply each part by 5. Then, add the results together."

After posing the query this way, the AI model gives the response step by step explaining its thought process.

Tasks that require logical reasoning or detailed explanations, such as solving math problems or complex queries can benefit from this technique. You see better results with this.

Just remember to add for your query, "explain step by step."

8. Chain of Density

This advanced prompt technique focuses on generating dense, information-rich responses by connecting related ideas and concepts and then asking AI Model to summarize.

Let us say we want to utilize AI for helping with a career gap in your resume.

In this method you increase the complexity for the AI model. You start with an idea, ask question, and then have follow-up question, you can add additional input, and have AI summarize for you multiple times. It is observed that by 5th round of summary, AI generally gives the best responses.

Example

Prompt1: "First, acknowledge the career gap between January 2022 and June 2023. Then, identify any relevant skills or experiences I gained during that time, such as taking online courses in digital marketing, volunteering as a web developer for a non-profit, and freelancing for small businesses. Next, explain how these experiences have contributed to my professional development and enhanced my skills in [mention relevant skill, e.g., web development, project management]. Finally, write a concise statement that addresses the career gap in a positive and proactive manner, emphasizing my commitment to continuous learning and skill development."

Prompt2: "First, recognize the 18-month career gap in my work history. Then, list the specific skills I focused on improving during that time, like [skill 1], [skill 2], and [skill 3]. Next, for each skill, provide a brief example of how I practiced or developed it. Then, write a short paragraph for my resume that explains how I used the time to enhance my professional abilities and stay current in my field."

Prompt3: "First, acknowledge the gap in my employment from [start date] to [end date]. Next, identify any personal development activities I engaged in during that time, such as [travel, caregiving, personal projects]. Then, explain how these experiences have contributed to my personal growth and developed transferable skills like [adaptability, empathy, problem-solving]. Finally, create a brief statement for my resume that frames the career gap as a period of personal growth and skill development, highlighting the value I bring to a potential employer."

Prompt4: "First, identify the career gap that represents my transition from [old field] to [new field]. Then, list the relevant courses, certifications, and projects I completed during this transition. Next, explain how these activities demonstrate my commitment to my new career path and the skills I gained. Finally, write a concise paragraph for my resume that explains my career transition and highlights my relevant skills and enthusiasm for the new field."

Prompt5: "First, acknowledge that my previous position was eliminated due to company downsizing. Then, list any relevant skills or experiences I gained during the time I was searching for new employment. Next, explain how this time was used to network, attend professional development events, and keep my skills current. Finally, create a statement for my resume that briefly explains the circumstances of my departure and emphasizes my proactive approach to finding new opportunities."

9.Tree of Thought

This technique involves structuring the prompt to guide the model through a decision tree, considering multiple branches and outcomes.

Complex decision-making tasks where multiple factors need to be evaluated systematically can use this prompt technique. This is similar to the way our brain's function.

This is most complex of the prompt engineering techniques. We will keep it brief.

An Example: "If you need to choose between A and B, consider the pros and cons of A: [list pros and cons]. Now consider the pros and cons of B: [list pros and cons]. Based on this, choose the best option."

Conclusion

I hope these 9 techniques will be a great addition to the way you obtain information from the AI generative tools. This is your own genie at hand. You must claim your position as the rightful master.

Chapter 15: Analytics, Automation & AIOps

Analytics

Imagine a vast ocean of data generated by IT infrastructure, user interactions, and service operations. Analytics provides the tools to navigate this data ocean, extracting valuable insights that guide informed decision-making within IT service delivery.

Data analysis can uncover patterns and trends that signal potential issues before they escalate into major incidents. Predictive analytics can identify anomalies in resource utilization, network performance, or user behaviour, allowing proactive intervention to prevent service disruptions.

By analysing service usage patterns and resource consumption, IT service delivery teams can optimize resource allocation. Analytics can reveal areas where resources are underutilized or oversubscribed, enabling more strategic resource allocation to meet service demands effectively.

Service level agreements (SLAs) define the performance expectations for IT services. Analytics helps monitor SLA compliance and identify areas where service delivery falls short of established benchmarks. This data-driven approach allows for continuous improvement of service levels and ensures customers receive the quality of service they expect.

Analytics can shed light on user behaviour patterns and service usage trends. By understanding how users interact with IT services, service delivery teams can personalize the service experience and tailor offerings to better meet user needs.

The Automation Advantage

Automation can fill role of a tireless worker who can work without breaks. By automating manual and repetitive tasks, service delivery teams can free up valuable time and resources to focus on higher-level activities.

Incident and Request Management: Automated workflows can handle routine tasks like incident ticketing, password resets, and service requests. This frees up service desk personnel to focus on complex issues and provide personalized support to customers.

Patch Management and System Updates: Automating patch deployment and system updates ensures timely security fixes and reduces the risk of vulnerabilities. This not only improves system security but also minimizes downtime associated with manual updates.

Configuration Management: Automated configuration management tools ensure consistency across IT infrastructure components, simplifying troubleshooting and reducing the risk of human error.

Self-Service Portals: Empowering users with self-service portals allows them to access knowledge bases, reset passwords, or request services independently. This reduces the burden on the service desk and provides users with 24/7 access to basic support functionalities.

AI Ops: The Rise of Artificial Intelligence in Service Delivery

AI Ops represents an evolution in IT service delivery leveraging machine learning algorithms to automate tasks, analyse data, and provide actionable insights.

It can analyze vast amounts of data to identify the root cause of incidents more quickly and accurately. This reduces the time spent troubleshooting and allows for faster resolution of service disruptions.

Event Correlation and Anomaly Detection: AI Ops can correlate events from various IT systems and identify anomalies that might signify potential problems. This proactive approach allows IT service delivery teams to address issues before they impact users.

Predictive Maintenance: By analysing historical data and user behaviour patterns, AI Ops can predict potential service disruptions or infrastructure bottlenecks. This enables proactive maintenance and resource optimization to prevent service outages.

Chatbots and Virtual Assistants: AI-powered chatbots and virtual assistants can provide basic support to users, answer frequently asked questions, and automate basic troubleshooting steps. This frees up service desk personnel to handle more complex issues and personalized interactions.

The Human-in-the-Loop Approach: Combining Automation with Expertise

While automation and AI offer significant benefits, human expertise is critical in IT service delivery. While automation can be a trusted approach, AI can never be completely relied upon as it has serious limitations, even with the best-advanced models. In service operations, we can use the AI services, but cannot implement all the recommendations received unless a Human is involved.

The most effective approach leverages both automation and human intelligence in a "human-in-the-loop" model.

Automation for Efficiency: **Repetitive tasks and data analysis are best suited for automation, freeing up human talent for critical decision-making and complex problem-solving.**

Human Expertise for Judgment and Insight: **Human judgment and expertise are essential for interpreting data-driven insights, making strategic decisions, and providing personalized support to customers. All the AI-generated recommendations should be screened by a human before implementation.**

Chapter 16: Conflict Resolution

While working as a Service delivery manager, our team and I worked an entire weekend to deliver a solution. The next morning, I received an escalation mail from the customer copying all our management team informing the work was not up to the mark.

I put all my energy into preparing a lengthy email, a strong point-by-point response. Before shooting the mail, showed the draft of the mail to my manager. He asked me to hold off the mail.

He then gave an excellent leadership titbit, if the customer sent an angry mail, it would mean that they are going through a tough situation and looking for help. Defending myself and the team's actions, will not solve their problem. Instead, he asked me to call the customer directly and understand the concern threadbare. He asked me to keep an open mind.

I called up the customer and had a long call. One of my team members communicated one thing to me and has done something else. There is a compliance issue. The customer was not willing to put this in the mail. The issue was entirely something else! We fixed it.

I had to close it with our internal management as well. I put together a 2,3-line email thanking the customer for the discussion that morning and that the issue is resolved. Only the customer is included in the email to-list, all my management moved to BCC on the mail so they all could see the closure without requiring them to respond further.

Had I responded via email immediately with a strong response, you could guess how it would have played out.

Conflict happens due to a lack of communication; my manager has been a wise person to stop me and guide me the right way. Conflict resolution requires effective communication and an open mind.

Conflict between Practice(functional) manager & Project manager

In a matrix organization, the project manager complained to me (The practice manager) that one of the resources allocated is not willing to work on a specific project.

This person is open to work on any other project except the one assigned. But would not explain why. The project manager took it as a personal insult. There were escalation calls between the project & practice teams. The project manager was adamant he needed the same person.

I met with a close colleague of this person and the issue was a surprise. The project is for a worldwide alcoholic beverages corp. This person due to religious beliefs, did not want to have anything to do with it.

Some issues are trivial, was lucky to find the root cause in this case, but you may never know sometimes. Once known, all the managers moved on, and I swapped projects of team members.

May not always work, but another fix for conflict resolution is empathy. Empathy helps resolve issues.

Conflict between two employees

The bifurcation of Andhra Pradesh, leading to the formation of Telangana as India's 29th state, was marked by significant emotional and political tension.

Two of my employees from each of these regions had an altercation. The language spoken in both these regions is same, but the slang & accents are different. One of the employees felt the other was insulting while other claimed it to be his way of speaking.

They should have resolved it themselves, somehow it came to me. There was no impact on their work performance, with both doing well. They had strong political views and it is not easy to resolve ideological differences.

As a short-term fix, I told them not to communicate in the native and henceforth speak either in English or Hindi. Warned that if there is any impact on the performance of the project, I could act.

Some conflicts are silly and in retrospective funny. Get creative!

Conflict resolution steps

Effective conflict resolution is a key part of being a leader. Disagreements happen, and it is up to you to manage them in a way that minimizes disruption and fosters a productive team environment. Few points of reference.

Address it Early: Do not let small issues fester. Intervene promptly to prevent escalation.

Gather Information: Talk to everyone involved individually to understand their perspectives.

Facilitate Discussion: Bring involved parties together to discuss the issue openly and honestly in a neutral environment.

Focus on Solutions: Work together to brainstorm solutions that address everyone's concerns.

Find Common Ground: Look for areas of agreement and build from there.

Compromise may be necessary: Sometimes the best solution involves concessions from all sides.

Follow-up: Monitor the situation to ensure the chosen solution is working and address any lingering issues.

In the next chapter, we will be discussing verbal & non-verbal communication skills in detail. Skills which are highly necessary for leaders.

Chapter 17: Non-Verbal Communication

There is a memory that stayed with me from a young age. Our class teacher has given us homework and asked us to submit it "Tomorrow". Being a non-native English speaker, that was the first time I heard that word and could not understand. The teacher was an Anglo-Indian lady who could not speak my native tongue.

I approach and ask her in my native language what I should do. She explains something and we cannot understand each other and I go back to my place.

Utterly confused, I could not sit and approach again, very brave for a small kid asking what to do. She wrote in a book and communicated through body gestures and I figured I must take this book to my mom.

This instance stayed with me throughout.

Communication, either words or gestures is so critical. Every person aspires to lead a happy & fun-filled life. This is done through the sharing of thoughts and feelings with others. The more we communicate, the less we suffer and the better we feel.

In this chapter, we will explore important non-verbal communication channels:

- Active Listening
- Non-Verbal
    - Body Language
    - Facial expressions
    - Tone & Voice

Active Listening Skills

Do not be surprised to see Listening being a communication skill. Active listening is the process of paying attention to the speaker, understanding their message, and responding thoughtfully. It is an essential skill for effective communication in all areas of life, from personal relationships to professional settings.

As famously quoted, God gave one mouth but 2 ears to speak less and hear more. Interestingly, ears cannot be shut so we can Listen all the time including during sleep. But are you an Active Listener?

There is a famous story about American President Abraham Lincoln. While legislating for slavery abolishment, Lincoln was having a tough time getting sufficient votes to pass. He wanted to clear his mind and have better clarity and spoke to his friend William Herndon about his thoughts and feelings.

Lincoln began to speak, and he spoke for a long time. He talked about Slavery, the sacrifices that the Union soldiers were making, the challenges that he was facing as president, and his hopes for the future of the country.

Herndon listened patiently to everything that Lincoln had to say. He did not interrupt, and he did not offer any advice. He simply listened. He listened for an entire evening.

When Lincoln was finished speaking, Herndon simply looked at him and said, "Thank you for sharing that with me."

Lincoln was grateful, he told Herndon that this was the best conversation he ever had, and now knew exactly what he should do.

We can see that this is no conversation. This is almost one-sided talk. But it is Active Listening on the part of Mr Herndon. One may ask, this benefits the other person, what will I get if I am an active listener?

When we listen actively, we show the other person that we care about them and that we value their thoughts and feelings. We can better understand the person and their concerns. We also give them the space they need to process their emotions and come to their conclusions.

Active listener is a much sought-after person, it is a great personality trait to possess. This will lead to building trust with the other person. Trust is the cornerstone of any relationship. Active listening is an important skill for everyone to have, especially for aspiring leaders.

Important notes on Active Listening

- While talking to others, be fully present. Put away your distractions, such as your phone, and give the speaker your full attention.
- Make eye contact and nod your head to show that you are listening.
- Pay attention to body language. Body language can communicate a lot about what someone is feeling, even if they are not saying it directly. Pay attention to the speaker's posture, facial expressions, and hand gestures.
- Ask clarifying questions. This shows that you are interested in what they have to say and you can understand them better.
- Avoid finishing their sentences
- Acknowledge speakers' emotions, ex: You sound excited/frustrated, etc.,
- Refrain from passing judgment or offering a solution too soon. Active listening is about understanding the other person's perspective, even if you don't agree with it

- Do not give your opinion or feedback unless asked. Sometimes, people just want to let out their thoughts, they do not need any further advice.

- Cultivate reading between the lines. What is not being said?

- Mind your body language: Convey you are open to what they have to say. In some cultures, having crossed arms can be considered as not being open to hearing their viewpoint, better to have arms uncrossed.

- Paraphrase what you have heard. This is a good way to check for understanding and to make sure that you are on the same page as the speaker. To paraphrase, simply repeat what the speaker has said in your own words.

- Be empathetic. Try to put yourself in the speaker's shoes and see things from their perspective. This will help you to better understand what they are saying and why they are saying it.

Reflect on your active listening skills. Improve through practice with friends or relatives. Ask for feedback from others if they feel you have heard them right and what are your areas of improvement. You will be surprised to hear the feedback, do not get offended, take it in the right stride.

Attending a communication workshop would also help improve this skill.

Non-Verbal Communication

There is a famous 7% Rule (Albert Mehrabian, 1971), which states that 93% of communication is non-verbal: 55% body language and 38%

through the tone or intonation of the voice and only 7% to the spoken word or the actual content.

We will not get into the actual merit of the exact percentage, but it is acknowledged that through Body language, facial expressions, and Tone we can communicate our thoughts, feelings, and intentions without saying a word. It includes our facial expressions, gestures, posture, Walking style, eye contact, tone of voice or a simple smile.

A personal experience

We faced a critical client visit with my manager, who had prepared the presentation, unexpectedly unavailable due to a personal matter. Despite several team members being available, including myself, none were familiar with the presentation.

With only a few hours' notice, our senior leader, whom I had not previously interacted with, asked me to present. Though I had limited time to prepare, I managed to deliver the presentation.

My manager later revealed, the only reason I was chosen because our senior leader felt I smiled more than the others!

This incident demonstrates how personality assessments, based on body language, can occur without our knowledge. We are consistently being observed and evaluated.

Effective body language can help us to build rapport, convey confidence, and make a positive impression on others.

We do not know who the audience is or who is judging us. But why not be prepared always? Put on the greatest show ever!

1. Body Language

Good posture communicates confidence and self-assurance. Try to remember any of your favourite celebrities and how they display this. Maintaining a good body posture daily is a good amount of effort. On practice, becomes our natural self.

Standing & Walking:

- Stand up straight and tall, with your shoulders back and relaxed.
- Keep your head level and in line with your spine.
- Tuck in your chin slightly.
- Pull in your abdomen.
- Keep your feet shoulder-width apart.
- Distribute your weight evenly on both feet.
- Do not slouch shoulders while walking
- Wall support: Stand with your back against a wall, with your feet shoulder-width apart and your head, shoulders, and hips touching the wall. Slowly slide down the wall and take a walk. Try getting back to the wall again with your back and check if you have maintained your posture. Ideally, you should always be walking with this correct posture. This also helps in the long run and has health benefits.
- Try to film yourself while practising. It may feel awkward initially. Give yourself some time and you will be there.

Sitting

- Sit up straight with your back supported by the chair.
- Keep your feet flat on the floor or a footrest.
- Keep your knees and hips at a 90-degree angle.
- Keep your elbows close to your sides and your wrists straight.

- If at a desk before a computer, have the monitor at eye level and your keyboard and mouse within easy reach.
- Here are some additional tips for maintaining good posture:
- Be mindful of your posture throughout the day. If you catch yourself slouching, gently correct your posture.
- Take breaks every 20-30 minutes to stand up and move around.
- Exercise regularly to strengthen your core muscles and improve your flexibility.
- Use ergonomic furniture and equipment to support your body when you are sitting or standing for long periods.
- Use Open gestures such as open palms and uncrossed arms, to communicate that you are approachable and friendly while sitting or standing. Avoid using closed gestures, such as crossed arms or fidgeting, as these can communicate that you are closed off or defensive.
- Mirror the other person's body language. This is a subconscious way of building rapport and trust.

Hand Shakes

Personally, this is one of the most important gestures to find the mood of the other person. If the handshake is very feeble, it shows they are not interested. If it is almost crushing, they are trying to impress upon or could suggest desperation. You can assess others, but why would you want others to assess you by a simple handshake? Practice this technique

- Make eye contact and smile. This shows that you are friendly and approachable.

- Grasp the other person's hand with a firm but gentle grip. Your grip should be firm enough to show that you are interested in meeting the other person, but not so firm that you crush their hand.

- Shake hands two or three times. Do not shake hands too vigorously or for too long.

- Release the other person's hand and step back.

Handshake mistakes to avoid

- The limp fish handshake. This handshake is weak and shows a lack of interest.

- The death grip handshake. This handshake is too firm and can be uncomfortable or even painful for the other person.

- The bone crusher handshake. This handshake is like the death grip handshake, but it is even more forceful and can hurt the other person.

- The overzealous handshake. This handshake is too enthusiastic and can make you seem pushy or aggressive.

- The one-handed handshake. This handshake is considered rude and disrespectful.

2. Body Language: Facial Expressions

Be mindful of your facial expressions. Your facial expressions can communicate a wide range of emotions, from happiness to sadness to anger. Make sure that your facial expressions are appropriate for the situation and that they convey the message that you want to send.

Be yourself. The most important thing is to be genuine and authentic. If you are trying too hard to be someone you are not, your facial expressions will show.

Smile

Smiling is a powerful tool; it creates a good impression. It can alter the outcomes of a course of events. I personally already narrated my own experience earlier and would give two more that I have closely observed.

A few years back somewhere in the 1990's watched a cricket match between India & South Africa. South Africa played well and set a decent score and India was batting next. Midway into the match, the Indian team did not lose a single wicket and scored two-thirds of the target.

The target is not far, everything going in favour, Indian team is winning. The pressure is showing on the South African team. Every team member is grim, the stakes are high and the loss means the team is out of the tournament. The pressure is showing on the fielders who are making mistakes. In one instance, a fielder made a mistake and South African team captain Hansie Cronje had a smile, almost like a hearty laugh with his other team members witnessing.

I was watching on television and could feel immediately; this will change the course of the match. Surprisingly, in the next few overs, the balance started shifting. Indian cricket team started losing wickets and finally lost.

One of the successful bowlers who took maximum wickets mentioned later in the interview that seeing the captain smile lifted his spirits and made him perform well.

Another instance is the general elections in India in 2014 fought between UPA & NDA. UPA has been in power for 10 years. Results were declared and UPA lost. There was a speech at which UPA chairperson Ms Sonia Gandhi has conceded defeat. Her son Mr Rahul Gandhi was seen smiling while she was speaking.

There is nothing inappropriate and it is just a simple smile. The next day, screaming news anchors and reports saying it was not appropriate to smile at that juncture.

The only reason to mention this is to show how a simple smile can impact the perspectives of others.

Effectively used, a smile can change an entire course of events!

- Smile genuinely. People can tell when you are faking a smile, so make sure your smile is genuine and comes from within.

- Smile with your eyes. A genuine smile engages the muscles around your eyes, causing them to crinkle slightly. This is known as a Duchenne smile, and it is the most trustworthy type of smile.

- Smile at the right time. Smiling all the time can make you seem fake or disingenuous. Save your smiles for when they are appropriate, such as when meeting someone new, greeting a friend, or giving a presentation.

- Smile at the right people. Smiling at strangers can be considered rude in some cultures. Be mindful of the cultural norms of the people you are interacting with before smiling.

- Smile with confidence. A confident smile will make you look more approachable and attractive. Hold your head high and make eye contact when you smile.

Ways to use a smile to your advantage

- Smile when you are networking. Smiling will make you seem more approachable and friendly, which can help you make new connections and build relationships.

- Smile when you are giving a presentation. Smiling will help you relax and project confidence, which will make your audience more likely to engage with your message.

- Smile when you are in customer service. Smiling will make customers feel welcome and valued.

- Smile when you are having a difficult conversation. Smiling can help to de-escalate the situation and make the conversation more productive.

- Smile when you are feeling down. Smiling can improve your mood and make you feel happier.

Eye Contact

Effective eye contact is an important skill for communication and personal interaction. It can help you to build rapport, show interest, and project confidence.

- Make eye contact before you start talking. This shows that you are paying attention and interested in what the other person has to say.

- Hold your gaze for 4-5 seconds at a time. This is the ideal amount of time to make eye contact without staring or making the other person uncomfortable.

- Use the triangle technique. This involves looking at the person's left eye, right eye, and mouth, then back to their left eye. This will help you to maintain eye contact without making it feel awkward.

- Blink naturally. Don't try to hold your gaze for so long that you forget to blink. This will make you look unnatural and nervous.

- Look away naturally. It's okay to look away occasionally, especially to break up a long sentence or to take a moment to think. Just be sure to look back at the person's eyes when you resume speaking.

Eye contact mistakes to avoid

- Darting eyes. Looking away too quickly can make you appear nervous or shy.

- Staring. Holding eye contact for too long can make the other person feel uncomfortable or intimidated.

- Avoiding eye contact altogether. This can make you appear uninterested or untrustworthy.

- Only make eye contact when you are talking. It is also important to make eye contact while you are listening. This shows that you are engaged in the conversation and that you care about what the other person has to say.

It is important to practice making eye contact in different situations. The more you practice, the more comfortable you will become at doing it.

Practicing eye contact

- Start by practising with people you know well. This will help you to feel more comfortable and confident.

- Once you feel more comfortable, start practising eye contact with strangers. This could be as simple as making eye contact with the cashier at the grocery store or the person sitting next to you on the bus.

- You can also practice eye contact in front of a mirror. This will help you to see how you look and to make sure that you are not staring.

With practice, you will be able to master the art of effective eye contact.

Facial expressions-Miscellaneous

Be aware of your cultural context. Different cultures have different norms and expectations when it comes to body language. For example, in some cultures, it is considered rude to make direct eye contact.

Pay attention to the other person's body language. This can help you to understand their thoughts, feelings, and intentions. For example, if someone is avoiding eye contact or crossing their arms, it may be a sign that they are uncomfortable or defensive.

Nod your head: Nodding your head shows that you are engaged in the conversation and that you are interested in what the other person has to say.

Proxemics

The concept of personal space and how it varies between individuals and cultures is proxemics. While speaking with another person, the distance between the two communicates Intimacy or discomfort. Different cultures have varying norms regarding personal space and touch. Do not get too close to a person while talking unless they are very close to you. Give sufficient space

3. Body Language: Tone

Tone or intonation is how something is said or written. Our minds are hardwired to quickly judge a person. You are conversing with a person. The intonation is confident and polished. Forget the content of the words being spoken, your view of the person changes.

The tone of a person can convey a speaker's or writer's attitude, emotion, or intent. Tone can be expressed through a variety of means, including word choice, sentence structure, punctuation, and body language.

For example, the following two sentences have different tones:

- "You need to finish your homework."
- "Can you please finish your homework?"

The first sentence has a more direct and commanding tone, while the second sentence has a more polite and respectful tone.

Tone can also be used to convey a speaker's or writer's sense of humour, irony, or sarcasm. For example, the following sentence could be used to express either surprise or sarcasm:

- "Oh, really? You are the expert on this topic?"

Examples of different tones:

- **Formal**: This tone is used in professional settings, such as in business letters and presentations. It is characterized by using proper grammar and vocabulary.

- **Informal**: This tone is used in casual conversations and personal letters. It is characterized using contractions and slang.

- **Humorous**: This tone is used to make people laugh. It is characterized using puns, jokes, and other forms of comedy.

- **Serious**: This tone is used to convey important information or to express strong emotions. It is characterized using direct language and a serious tone of voice.

- **Angry**: This tone is used to express anger or frustration. It is characterized using harsh language and a loud tone of voice.

- **Sad**: This tone is used to express sadness or grief. It is characterized using soft language and a slow tone of voice.

It is important to be aware of the tone of your messages, both when speaking and writing. By using the appropriate tone, you can communicate your message more effectively and build better relationships with others.

Practice exercises

Effective communication is a skill that takes time and practice to develop. But by following a few exercises, you can start to improve.

- Record yourself talking. This will help you to see how your facial expressions, body language & tone look to others.
- Get feedback from a trusted friend or family member. Ask them to let you know if your facial expressions, body language & tone are congruent with your message.
- Practice in front of a mirror. This will help you make sure that you are not exaggerating.

- The Power of Handshakes: Practice a firm handshake with close friends or partners
- Analysing Famous Public Figures' Body Language
- Break down the body language of well-known individuals in various contexts.
- Role-Playing Exercises for Practicing Effective Body Language
- Nonverbal Cues in Leadership and Professional Success
- Practice various scenarios of body language for leadership, job interviews, and career advancement before a mirror.
- Using Hand and Arm Gestures to Convey Messages or clarify spoken words
- Speak in a clear and confident voice, and avoid using a monotone voice.

Chapter 18: Communication- Verbal

I took up an advanced mathematics course as part of my Master's degree. Our professor at the university is an interesting person. He would wear the same clothes every single day.

In the first session, he explained a few simple concepts. They were as simple as at the 5th or 6th grade level. We were Master's graduates and this course is called Advanced Mathematics!

For the second session, all the students were cracking jokes wondering if he would wear a different pair of clothes and if he would advance to the next grade.

The professor arrived, Starts with couple of simple tasks. Then, a few minutes into, tougher concepts start rolling in. It gets tougher and tougher and he is navigating so smoothly. Handling any questions, explaining. We were in Awe!

All my friends gathering on the university lawn after class, could not stop praising. What great communication, What a genius, What clarity of thought. *What a great Professor!*

You have a quick judgement about someone on appearance. And then, they start speaking, What an extraordinary person! You may wonder! and your entire perspective changes.

Verbal communication can be developed with Practice. Either Spoken or Written.

Spoken verbal communication

- One on One conversation
    - Face to face
    - Phone calls
    - Video calls
- Presentations
- Public Speaking

Written verbal communication

- Emails
- Text messages,
- Social media posts
- Letters

The CASE Method: How to start a conversation?

There is a great method I suggest--**CASE**. In my observation, this works well. You can certainly make customizations.

Compliment----Ask Question ---- Set context ----Educate

Compliment: Start any conversation or meeting with a compliment or appreciation. People like it. Compliment is not flattery. Keep it short and it needs to be genuine. If you cannot find a good compliment, just stick with a simple, thanks for taking my call or appreciate taking some time of yours!

Ask Question: After a compliment, what people like most, is to talk, mostly about themselves. Give them an opportunity. This is always a good icebreaker. If you cannot find a good question to ask, just stick with the simple 'How are you doing?'

Set context: Now let the other person or group know, why are you talking to them. Give the context, in a minute or two. Always keep this short. Context should not be a 30-minute speech. You can expand later.

Educate: Now that you have the ice broken, give the Gyan (Knowledge)! Educate the other person or group on the actual content. Spend time here and keep it interactive.

CASE method is an excellent way to start a conversation and it is followed by the most successful speakers and leaders. Once you get started, a few other important points

- Clarity: Use clear and concise language that is easy for the listener to understand. Do not use difficult-to-understand words, use the simplest of words. Remember, the purpose is to have another person understand what you are trying to communicate. Never to show off.

- Conciseness: Get to the point quickly and avoid unnecessary rambling

- Accuracy: Provide accurate information and avoid making false statements

- Appropriateness: Use language and a tone of voice that are appropriate for the setting and the audience

- Engagement: Use voice, body language, and facial expressions to engage the audience and keep them interested

- Active listening: As already covered in an earlier chapter, be an active listener and pay attention to what the other person is saying.

How to improve verbal communication

Verbal communication exercises are needed for improvement. Unfortunately, a book cannot do complete justice here. I would mention a few points, but a good public speaking course that would cover various scenarios would be required to get better at this skill. Few important points.

- Practice speaking regularly: The more you practice speaking, the more confident and comfortable you will become.

- Get feedback: Ask others to give you feedback on your speaking skills. This can help you to identify areas where you need to improve.

- Record yourself speaking: This can help you to identify areas where you need to improve, such as your tone of voice, body language, and use of language.

- Join a Toastmasters club: Toastmasters is an international organization that helps people to improve their public speaking and leadership skills.

- Take a public speaking class: Choose a course where you can either be in person or over a web meeting. Towards the end of this book, there are further details on a public speaking course as well.

- Body language: Be aware of your body language and tone of voice. Make eye contact with your audience, stand up straight, and use gestures to emphasize your points. Speak clearly and slowly, and use variety in your voice.

- Tailor your message to your audience: Consider the audience's interests, knowledge level, and cultural background when choosing your language and content.

Communication over the phone or Video

After the COVID pandemic, work-from-home culture has increased across organizations. Some workplaces do not have any physical conversations anymore. Communication over the phone or video is now a skill and this special section is for you.

The Preparation

Before you start a video or phone call, take a few minutes to prepare. Think about what you want to say and how you want to say it. This will help you to be clear and concise in your communication.

- Test your equipment before the call. Make sure that your microphone and camera (if using video) are working properly.
- Find a quiet place to talk. This will help to reduce background noise and make your voice easier to hear.
- Avoid distractions. Close any unnecessary tabs or programs on your computer and turn off your phone.
- Smile. Even though the other person cannot see you, smiling can help to make your voice sound more friendly and engaging.
- Take breaks. If you are on a long call, take breaks to stand up and move around. This will help to keep you focused and engaged.

Be aware of your body language

Even though the other person cannot see you, your body language can still have an impact on your communication. It has been researched that if you speak the same way you speak on a phone as that in a direct physical conversation, the other person can receive it as such. For example, if you have a mild smile on your face while speaking, even if it is just a phone call, it was observed that the other person could sense it over the phone.

When speaking over video or phone, try to sit up straight and maintain eye contact with the camera or in the case of the phone have a good body posture. This will help you to project confidence and engagement.

Speak clearly and slowly

It is important to speak clearly and slowly when communicating over video or phone. This can help to avoid misunderstandings.

Use pauses: Pauses can be an effective way to emphasize important points and give the other person a chance to process what you are saying.

Be enthusiastic: Even though you are not communicating face-to-face, it is important to show enthusiasm when speaking over video or phone. This will help to engage the other person and make the conversation more enjoyable.

Presentations: If you are giving a presentation or training session over video, have a visual aid such as PowerPoint slides or screen sharing. People can connect better visually. Just have a few simple slides. This can help to engage the audience and make your presentation more informative and interesting.

2. Written communication

Written skill differs from spoken verbal communication in a few important ways. First, written verbal communication is more deliberate and thoughtful than spoken verbal communication.

Second, written communication can be edited and revised before it is sent to the recipient.

Third, written verbal communication can be stored and referenced later.

Written verbal communication is used in a variety of settings, both personal and professional. Some common examples of written verbal communication include:

- Emails
- Letters
- Reports
- Proposals
- Presentations
- Social media posts
- Text messages

How to draft an effective email or a report:

Some of these points could be repetition of spoken communication as well. An important point is to distinguish written communication in a personal and professional context. Some of us have started using informal communication as part of professional context as well. This is a strict no.

For example:" How r u?" is ok in an informal context, but when you do in a professional setting, it needs to be a proper "How are you?"

Organization

Logically organize the information so that the reader can easily follow the main points.

- Know your audience. Consider the audience's interests, knowledge level, and cultural background when choosing your language and content.
- Tailor your message to your audience. Avoid using jargon or technical language that your audience may not understand.
- Be specific. Avoid using vague or general language. Instead, be as specific as possible when conveying your message.
- Use strong verbs. Verbs are the workhorses of any sentence. Choose strong verbs to make your writing more dynamic and engaging.
- Accuracy: Provide accurate information and avoid making false statements.
- Vary your sentence structure. Avoid using the same sentence structure repeatedly. This can make your writing boring and predictable.

Proofreading

Proofread the document carefully to catch any errors in grammar, spelling, or punctuation. Make sure to send it only after you do the below

- Read widely. The more you read, the better your understanding of language and grammar will become.

- Write regularly. The more you write, the better you will become at expressing yourself clearly and concisely.

- Get feedback from others. Ask others to read your writing and give you feedback. This can help you to identify areas where you need to improve.

- Use a grammar checker. A grammar checker can help you to catch errors in grammar, spelling, and punctuation.

Chapter 19: Time Management

Just a month after my marriage, I have a funny recollection of meeting a couple. They both congratulated me and my wife on our marriage and both recollected their own marriage 2 years ago. Both said almost at the same time:

"Feels like yesterday" -The husband said

"Two long years! -The wife said

I and my wife recollect this event to this day and laugh at the way both the husband and wife felt the passage of the 2 years since their marriage. Even though the time allocated to each of the human beings is finite, due to our minds, it seems stretchable.

Let me ask you to remember any memorable vacation you have taken. The day would seem beautiful, and exciting. Another day which is just normal. You would have observed that the duration of those days in recollection seems different.

Time management is a mindset. If you can learn and implement time management effortlessly, life will be more enjoyable. Let me also warn of a pitfall here. Some take time management too seriously and try to have everything according to the clock. Balance is the key.

A personal experience

My own experience with time management has been in a rude way. I had an assignment which I could not complete and my teacher was not happy about it. I was later complaining to our class topper who would always do everything on time. Told him, I did not get sufficient time to complete this work. He replied, "I too only have 24 hours in a day!"

He is a proud and arrogant type of person so sure about himself. But over the years, his statement remained with me. Even today, if I find myself short of time for anything, I just remember that sentence and the way he said it to me. Gets me all fired up!

We all have the same amount of time. Then, how is it that some accomplish more and some less?

Introduction to time management

Time management is the process of planning and controlling how much time we spend on specific activities. Good time management improves our productivity, reduces stress, and gives a greater satisfaction at the end of the day.

If we can wake up and sleep a happy person, what more would we want?

- Increased productivity: When you manage your time effectively, you can get more done in a shorter period. This can lead to increased productivity at work or school, as well as more free time to enjoy hobbies and interests.

- Reduced stress: When you feel overwhelmed by your workload, it can lead to stress and anxiety. Good time management can help you reduce stress by giving you a sense of control over your time and your to-do list.

- Improved performance: When you have a good time management system in place, you can focus on your tasks and complete them to a high standard. This can lead to improved

performance at work or school, as well as a sense of accomplishment.
- Greater satisfaction: When you can manage your time effectively and achieve your goals, it can lead to increased satisfaction with your life.

Time management techniques

Luckily for us, we do not need to reinvent the wheel. There has been some good research and we will focus on the Eisenhower Decision matrix.

In the book "The 7 Habits of Highly Effective People." Author Stephen Covey credited President Eisenhower for the idea but refined and promoted it in his work. So, while it is linked to Eisenhower, it is Covey who is often cited as the one who brought it into the mainstream.

Let us divide all tasks and activities based on their urgency and importance. It is a 2x2 grid, with the following quadrants:

- **Fire Fighting(Q1)**: Urgent and Important: These are tasks that need to be done immediately, such as a fire drill or a deadline for a critical project.
- **Productive(Q2)**: Not Urgent but Important: These are tasks that are important but not urgent, such as planning for a future project or learning a new skill.
- **Distraction(Q3)**: Urgent but Not Important: These are tasks that are urgent but not important, such as answering a phone call from a salesperson or responding to a non-urgent email.
- **Waste(Q4)**: Not Urgent and Not Important: These are tasks that are neither urgent nor important, such as watching TV or browsing social media.

Time Management Quadrants

	Urgent	Not Urgent
Improtant	**Q1: Fire Fighting** Emergencies Crises Deadlines	**Q2: Productive** Planning, Strategy, Relationship building, Entertainment, Vacation
Not Important	**Q3: Distraction** Seemingly Important: Emails, Phone calls, Meetings	**Q4: Wastage** Social media, Television, Etc.,

To use the Time Management Matrix, list your tasks in the appropriate quadrant. Once you have listed them, you can start to prioritize them.

Q1: Necessity tasks should be done immediately. These are the most important tasks, and they need to be completed right away.

Q2: Productive tasks should be scheduled for later. These tasks are important, but they are not urgent. You can schedule them for a time when you have more time to work on them.

Q3: Distraction tasks should be delegated to someone else. These tasks are urgent but not important, so you can delegate them to someone else who has more time to work on them.

Q4: Waste tasks should be eliminated or postponed. These tasks are neither urgent nor important, so you can eliminate them or postpone them.

Note: Our goal should be to focus and remain as much time as possible in Quadrant 2. These are the activities that will help us achieve our long-term goals and objectives. This means spending time on things like planning, learning, and building relationships. Quadrant 2 activities are often not urgent, but they are very important.

Our focus on Quadrant 2 over a period will reduce Quadrant 1 activities

How to use this matrix

1. List all your tasks

2. Give priority to tasks based on "Necessity, Productive, Distraction & Waste"

3. Write down each of these tasks in the above matrix

- Be realistic about how much time you have. Do not overload yourself with too many tasks in Quadrant 1.
- Be flexible. Things do not always go according to plan, so be prepared to adjust your priorities as needed.
- Review your Time Management Matrix regularly. Your priorities may change over time, so it is important to review your matrix regularly and adjust as needed.
- Set goals and priorities: What do you want to achieve in the short term and long term? Once you know your goals, you can prioritize your tasks and focus on the most important ones.
- Plan your time: Once you have prioritized your tasks, create a plan for how you will spend your time. This will help you to stay on track and avoid distractions.
- Break down large tasks: Large tasks can be daunting and overwhelming. Break them down into smaller, more

manageable tasks. This will make them seem less daunting and help you to make progress.

- Set deadlines: Deadlines will help you to stay on track and avoid procrastination.

- Take breaks: Frequent breaks few minutes each will help you to stay focused and productive.

- Delegate tasks: If possible, delegate. This will free up your time so that you can focus on the most important tasks.

Punctuality

Showing respect for others and their time is a valued quality in both personal and professional life. Punctuality demonstrates that you are reliable and trustworthy.

- When on time, you are less likely to be stressed. This allows you to focus on your tasks and to get more done.

- Punctuality can help build stronger relationships. This can help you to build stronger relationships with your friends, family, and colleagues.

Let us say a manager calls for the 10-member team to meet. It is scheduled at 10 am but he arrives by 10:05. There is a wastage of 50-minute collective team time. Even small misses like this can add up.

There are a couple of important points concerning Punctuality

Attitude: Time management, is not to be based on the importance of events, it is an attitude to be developed. Giving priority to someone or some events and ignoring others based on their importance is a bad practice.

Expectation: Always have realistic expectations. Do not try to cram too much into one day. Be realistic about how much time you have and how long each task will take. It is better to plan an event or meet later than to miss or be late.

People like certainty. They will be more than happy if the expectation is set and communicated properly.

Procrastination

Procrastination, the act of delaying or postponing tasks can have different reasons.

Some procrastinate because they are afraid of failure or the task to be overwhelming. Others procrastinate because they are perfectionists or because they have difficulty managing their time. For some others, it just could be that they are simply lazy.

Whatever the case, procrastination can hurt our productivity and well-being. Few tips

- Break down large tasks into smaller, more manageable steps.
- Set deadlines for yourself and stick to them.
- Reward yourself for completing tasks on time.
- Avoid distractions when you are trying to work.
- If you find yourself procrastinating, take a short break and come back to the task later.

Appendix: Noble Virtues

Leaders are observed and followed. Great leaders are appreciated for their Virtues.

The noble virtues are a set of qualities that have been cherished by people of all cultures and religions throughout history. Virtues are important because they help us to be better people. They help us to make good choices. They help develop a better personality.

Virtues can be learned and developed through practice. For example, a person who wants to be courageous will stand up for what he or she believes in, even when it is unpopular. A forgiving person will let go of anger and resentment even when someone has wronged them.

The virtues we seek are often already within us, waiting to be revealed. Like a diamond, they need only polishing. The simple resolve to integrate them into our lives will unlock their full potential.

Meditation

Humans are very close to the animal kingdom, except in the consciousness. We seem almost the only species that possess this. There are some reports of whales, dolphins, and a few others to a certain extent, but no other species at the level of Humans. This consciousness is both a boon and a bane for humans.

For any animal, there is no constant worry of happiness. It can relax if proper food, and shelter are provided. We are not like that. Even when provided with food, clothing, shelter, and every other basic need, we can worry. Humans can worry about the past by accessing their memories or use imagination to worry about future.

Our mind is going against us by remaining in the past or future. Meditation every morning 15 minutes a day can help remain in the present moment. This helps with sharper focus throughout the day and can help tasks performed in a shorter period. Alternatively, prayer also helps.

Continuous Learning

Our mind records everyday learnings and uses sleep to store all the memories of the day. The mind stays active and sends the body positive signals if it is having some exciting learning every day. As incredible as it sounds, this is a daily process throughout our lives.

We need to keep our minds engaged and make learning a lifelong journey. There is always more to learn and new skills to develop. By embracing continuous learning, you can ensure growth. It is an important part of personal development, as it allows us to keep up with the ever-changing world around us and to reach our full potential.

- Seek feedback from others about yourself. Do not be offended if they give bad feedback. Remember it is you who asked for it and take it genuinely and try to see if there is something you need to change or learn.
- Invest in yourself; Make learning a priority. Schedule some time each day or week to learn something new.
    - There are many ways to engage in continuous learning. Some people choose to take formal classes or workshops, while others prefer to learn independently through books, articles, and online resources.

- - Find a learning buddy or community. Learning with others can be more motivating and enjoyable.
- Learn from your mistakes: Do not be afraid to fail. Everyone makes mistakes when they are learning. View failure as an opportunity to learn and grow.
- Celebrate your successes. It is important to recognize and celebrate your accomplishments, both big and small.

There is no right or wrong way to learn, if you are trying.

Keep Learning, and Keep growing!

Relationship Building & Networking

Relationship building and networking are important skills for both personal and professional success. Strong relationships can provide us with emotional support, companionship, and growth opportunities. Networking can help us to find new job opportunities, learn new things, and expand our professional reach.

- Be genuine and interested in others.
- Be a good listener.
- Be supportive and helpful.
- Be reliable and trustworthy.
- Follow up with people after you meet them.

De-clutter & Organize

De-cluttering and organizing can help to reduce stress, improve productivity, and create a more peaceful and harmonious environment.

We have so much stuff that we do not need at our homes and on our office desks. Believe me, the clutter you see around also clutters your mind. Allocate sometime. Clean it up

- Start by getting rid of anything that you no longer use or need.
- Create a system for organizing your belongings.
- Put things away as soon as you are finished using them.
- Make de-cluttering and organizing a regular part of your routine.

Courage

There is a famous incident I heard in various forms. A professor asked her students to write an essay on the topic of Courage. She informed all the students that it is the most important test which will decide their grades. When she got to correct the answer sheets, found one of the student answer sheets to contain only two words in the otherwise completely blank sheet.

It read "This is"!

The professor gave an A+ to this student.

Courage is the strength to do what is right, even when it is difficult. It is the ability to face our fears and to stand up for what we believe in.

Courage is important because it allows us to overcome challenges and achieve our goals. It also allows us to protect the people and things that we care about.

- Identify your fears. What are the things that you are afraid of? Once you know what your fears are, you can start to develop strategies for overcoming them.

- Set small goals for yourself. Start by doing things that are slightly outside of your comfort zone. As you become more comfortable, you can gradually increase the difficulty of your challenges.

- Find a role model. Look for someone who embodies courage and who inspires you. Pay attention to how they handle themselves in difficult situations.

- Practice courage every day. Even small acts of courage can add up over time.

Generosity

One way to explain the positive effects of generosity is through the lens of hormones. When we are generous, our bodies release several hormones that have positive effects on our personality.

For example, when we give to others, our bodies release oxytocin, which is often referred to as the "love hormone." Oxytocin has been shown to have several positive effects, including reducing stress, increasing feelings of trust and empathy, and promoting social bonding.

Another hormone that is released when we are generous is dopamine, which is known as the "feel good" hormone. Dopamine plays a role in motivation, reward, and learning. When we give to others, we experience a dopamine hit, which reinforces the behaviour and makes us more likely to be generous in the future.

The research is still early, but it is becoming increasingly evident that being generous is helping with a better personality.

Generosity is the willingness to give our time, resources, and talents to others. It is the desire to help others and to make the world a better place.

There are many ways to be generous.

- Donate to charities that support causes that you care about.
- Volunteer your time to help others.
- Mentor someone less fortunate than you are.
- Give gifts to your friends and family.
- Be generous with your time and attention when someone mentions a problem, all you need to do is hear them out!

Forgiveness

Forgiveness is needed to let go of anger and resentment from the past. It is the ability to move on from past hurts and to start anew. Forgiveness is important because it allows us to heal from our emotional wounds.

Desmond Tutu a South African Anglican cleric was also a leading advocate for forgiveness and reconciliation. He believed that forgiveness was essential for healing the wounds of apartheid and building a better future for South Africa.

One of Tutu's most famous quotes is: "Forgiveness is not condoning what has happened to us. It is not saying that nothing wrong was done. It is not excusing the perpetrators of the wrong. Forgiveness is saying that, as a victim, I will not allow an offender to control me by continuing to make me angry or bitter."

Do not forget what has happened in your past. Take that as a lesson. It is a lesson life has taught us. Consider the past as education and move on.

Gratitude

Gratitude is the appreciation for the good things in our lives. It is the ability to recognize and appreciate the people, things, and experiences that make our lives better.

When I was very young, around 7 years of age, we were on a boat trip on a river along with a few other families. My dad bought a new suitcase just before the journey. We got down near a small river island for lunch and struggled to open the suitcase which was stuck. An old gentleman came over and tried to help. It did not work and went away after some time. My dad finally figured it out. New technology at that time, the suitcase was not supposed to be upside down.

My dad then asked me to go and inform the older gentleman that it was now open and thank him for his help. I remember asking my dad why tell him, we opened it ourselves. What he said that day remained with me throughout my life. "Always acknowledge even the smallest helpful gesture by others."

I then walked to that older gentleman and told him what happened and he was so happy to hear it. I could still remember his face glowing like all his problems were solved. Only as I grew older, I could understand this instance. In a single word, Gratitude.

Take time to appreciate the little things. It is easy to get caught up in the big things in life, but it is important to take time to appreciate the little things as well. Notice the beauty of a flower, the taste of your favourite food, or the sound of your loved ones' laughter.

Express your gratitude to others. Let the people in your life know how much you appreciate them. You can do this verbally, in writing, or through small acts of kindness.

Tolerance

Tolerance is the willingness to accept people and their beliefs, even if they are different from our own. It is the ability to live in peace and harmony with people from all walks of life.

Tolerance helps us to be open-minded. Which is needed for new ideas and perspectives. There is nothing wrong with having a certain preference for religion or ideas. But, always have the open-mindedness to accept that there are other ways different from our own.

Educate yourself about different cultures and religions. The more we know about others, the more likely we are to be tolerant of them. Be respectful of others, even if you disagree with them. Everyone is entitled to their own opinion.

Contentment

Let me leave you all with this final thought. My grandfather was a wise & knowledgeable man. He worked with Mahatma Gandhiji during India's freedom struggle and donated his possessions to the country.

I went to bid farewell to him for my master's degree in US. He never gave any advice to anyone. He felt everyone must learn by themselves. He was already in his 90s and was unsure if he would ever see me again, and imparted this beautiful word of wisdom.

All that a human being must achieve in their lives is "***Santhushtti***" (a Sanskrit word that most closely translates as Contentment).

Leaders are very ambitious people. Ambition, however, has a brother. It is called Sacrifice. They make many sacrifices to achieve what they believe in. A fine balance is needed. Whenever I lose my balance, I remember these beautiful words of wisdom.

Contentment gives the feeling of satisfaction and peace with one's life. Let go of expectations. Simplify your life. Do your best, accept circumstances, and find joy in the simple things of life.

The noble virtues discussed in this chapter are gifts we can give to ourselves and the world. By developing the noble virtues, we can make the world a better place, one person at a time.

God Bless you and your families.

I wish you, Health, Wealth, Wisdom, and Happiness.

---------------------------------------The End---------------------------------------

Acknowledgement

This effort would not have been possible if not for my wife Padma Sirisha who is a fierce critic and reviewer of my writings. Thank you Dear!

About the author

Bhaskar Challa is a Senior IT Services Leader and a Leadership, Career & Personality development Coach.

Bhaskar is Certified with Franklin Covey foundation, Dale Carnegie Organization Leadership Management Development Programs and has 25+ years of experience in Senior Leadership roles managing Mission critical projects, Revenue & People (Wissen Infotech, Oracle, Infosys, Capgemini, Genpact, WinWire, Suneratech etc.,). A Masters graduate in Computer Engineering from United states, and an MBA in Finance.

Bhaskar is associated with various Spiritual organizations: Art of Living, Isha Foundation, Vipassana, Heartfulness, Brahma Kumaris. A firm believer in human spirit, personally strives to be the best version of himself and tries to help others realize their best.

Contact

Website   :https://www.zmantra.blogspot.com
Youtube   :Youtube.com/@Zmantra
Twitter   :ZmantraOrg
Instagram   :ZmantraOrg
Facebook   :facebook.com/Zmantra
Linkedin   :Linkedin.com/company/Zmantra
Email   :Bhaskar.Challa@Zmantra.com

Books by Author

Distracted, But Determined

A book on Personality Development which aims to help individuals become a better version of themselves, while addressing solution for a very important issue -Distractions & addiction.

https://www.amazon.com/dp/B0CWS4Z1JF

IT Services Leadership Handbook

A one-stop guide to leadership development, tailored for Individuals moving into leadership roles. Helps to gain understanding of four major IT Service Leadership roles -Project, Program, Service Delivery & Practice management.

https://www.amazon.com/dp/B0D3BHLRK8

Landing Job in 40 Days

There is a great saying, do what you love and you would never have to work a single day in life. This book focuses on landing that Dream Job, the one a person loves to do, along with the AI prompt engineering job search techniques and a 40-day plan.

https://www.amazon.com/dp/B0DZP4KZ5V

www.ingramcontent.com/pod-product-compliance
Lightning Source LLC
Chambersburg PA
CBHW031434210526
45464CB00005B/2201